POCKET GUIDE TO

S

KATHLEEN S.

BOOK FAITH INDIA
Delhi

POCKET GUIDE TO THE 12 STEPS

Published by
BOOK FAITH INDIA
414-416 Express Tower
Azadpur Commercial Complex
Delhi, India 110033
Tel. [91-11] 713-2459. Fax [91-11] 724-9674
E-mail: pilgrim@del2.vsnl.net.in

Distributed by
PILGRIMS BOOK HOUSE
P.O. Box 3872
Kathmandu, Nepal
Tel. [977-1] 424942. Fax [977-1] 424943.
E-mail: pilgrims@wlink.com.np
WebSite: www.pilgrimsbooks.com

Varanasi Branch
PILGRIMS BOOK HOUSE
B 27/98-A-8, Durga Kund
Varanasi, India 221001
Tel. [91-542] 314060. Fax [91-542] 314059, 312788
E-mail: pilgrim@lw1.vsnl.net.in

All rights reserved
First Book Faith India Edition, 2000
Originally published by The Crossing Press, Inc. in 1997
Printed with permission from the publisher

ISBN 81-7303-223-8

Printed in India

CONTENTS

Introduction 5

Step One 11

Step Two 21

Step Three 27

Step Four 37

Step Five 49

Step Six 61

Step Seven 68

Step Eight 73

Step Nine 81

Step Ten 89

Step Eleven 98

Step Twelve 108

Resources 118

Introduction

For those who make the commitment to the 12-Step method, joyful living is a central goal. We seek to discover and explore our real selves. As we are able to do this, we find that we can establish healthy boundaries and make realistic commitments. The work we do on ourselves is meant to be applied in our present lives. Recovery isn't theoretical. It's practical. We seek always to practice these principles in our daily lives, not just to study them.

We come to the 12-Step programs for help and information. Personal pain brings us. Sometimes we are pressured to come because of family problems, maybe even trouble with the boss, or with the law. We may expect to be lectured at 12-Step meetings. Perhaps we anticipate short-term therapy that will give us insight to take back to our regular way of life.

The atmosphere at 12-Step meetings may come as a surprise. The experience of being welcomed by a room full of strangers may have felt unreal, a bit hard to trust. If we persist, however, after a few meetings most of us begin to feel more at home. We begin to identify with others and to see how our problems are similar to theirs. As we become more relaxed, we begin to uncover feelings we may not have known we had. In sharing, we come to find ourselves accepted, perhaps even understood.

Some of us initially fear being cramped into spiritual pigeonholes (the 12 Steps). The Steps may seem, at first, more of a challenge than a help. Even the slogans and friendly invitations to keep coming back may prompt memories of empty platitudes spoken in the past which were used to dismiss legitimate needs and feelings.

The emphasis on the Steps and the friendly encouragement that's common at meetings aren't intended to dismiss or minimize anyone's personal issues or feelings. 12-Step programs emphasize the Steps because they are a time-proven, neutral framework for the healing process. By applying the Steps to our issues, we are able to give each other respectful, individual support. Without giving advice or caretaking each other, we simply share the ways we have been able to relate the Steps to our own lives and problems. In so doing, we share our experience, strength, and hope with each other. We take what we find helpful from what is shared and leave the rest.

The trust within a group usually influences how individuals relate to the program. A move to a new community or group can create a need to re-bond and re-evaluate our whole outlook on recovery. Changes within a group's membership may have a similar impact.

For some, the bonding cycle is gradual. For others, it is characterized by dramatic shifts in how they relate to the program and program members. Some leave the program entirely, either permanently or temporarily, to resume their old lifestyle or to attempt recovery by another approach. Experimenters who do this and then return are often free of the inner reservations that before may have made the 12 Steps seem unnecessary or outdated. Those who choose to leave, for whatever reason, are free to return. Program participation is always a matter of personal decision.

Socializing and service work usually become more satisfying—and more balanced—as we integrate the 12-Step approach into our ways of relating to others. Often we become better able to accept praise and success. Authority issues may fall into more comfortable perspective. The Steps provide a path to free us gradually of insecurity in our relationships. We rarely become "boring and glum" when we make a commitment to the Steps.

Whatever issues bring us to a 12-Step fellowship, we are welcome in most groups if we say we are a member. Whatever phase of membership we are in today, be it "Breakthrough," "Just Shopping," "Pink Cloud," "Burn Out," or "Gradual Progress," we have a right to our perspective. We see our position as valid, as an important part of our growth. We have a right to be who we are. We have a right to all of our feelings. We also have a right to heal and to belong.

Some people move through the Steps in numerical order. Others find they prefer to jump around, surveying and getting a feeling for the Steps, answering their own questions about the way the program fits together before they actually work the Steps. If you are apprehensive about a Step, it is a good idea to risk investigating that Step first. If you find the wording of the Steps difficult to relate to, consider some alternative wording that you find more acceptable. It's up to you; there is no wrong way to work the Steps.

When you feel ready to make a commitment to your recovery which includes working the Steps, consider asking someone to sponsor (or co-sponsor) you. A sponsor should inspire respect in you. Usually, prospective sponsors are people who have found some measure of (day-at-a-time) relief from their own compulsions as a result of integrating the Steps into their own lives.

If you wish to have someone sponsor you, you must ask the person if s/he is willing to take on that responsibility. Some groups may have a list of individuals who are willing to be sponsors. Talk to the person before or after a meeting, or on the phone. If s/he is willing to sponsor you, establish some ground rules for working together: how often you will meet or speak on the phone, how much time you will spend on each Step, whether or not you will attend some meetings together, etc.

Co-sponsorship relationships are networks of individuals who are committed to working a 12-Step program together. There are many kinds of co-sponsorship arrangements. It may be two people who agree to support each other and share with each other, keeping the 12 Steps as a focus. Or co-sponsorship may include people with varying amounts of program experience, people of different ages, genders, ethnic backgrounds, or sexual orientations. Sometimes, co-sponsors may be members of a Step Study group which meets to read, discuss, and possibly journal through the 12 Steps.

Working Step 5 requires talking to someone you trust. It is possible to work Step 5 with a therapist or minister if s/he is familiar with the 12 Steps and feels the method is a valuable component in recovery from addictions and addiction-like problems.

All of the materials and techniques contained in this book are compatible with the principles and practices of the original 12-Step program, which credited innovative thinkers, including Dr. Carl Jung, for inspiration. Much concern has been given in this book to keeping alive the open-minded spirit which has made the 12-Step programs so vital and effective a force for healing. By crediting those who have added so much to our insight into the dynamics of chemical dependency and co-dependency, we have only continued a process of grateful acknowledgment that goes back to the earliest roots of the 12-Step programs.

Bill W., co-founder of Alcoholics Anonymous, advocated cooperation with professionals, "…we [in A.A.] regard all who labor in the total field of alcoholism as our companions on a march from darkness into light. We see that we can accomplish together what we could never accomplish in separation and rivalry." Dr. Bob, A.A.'s other co-founder, was an active force in designing effective approaches to alcoholism treatment, and many concepts of modern chemical dependency and co-dependency treatment remain indebted to these pioneering efforts in the infancy of the 12-Step programs.

Religious and spiritual tolerance, too, is a central feature in all 12-Step programs. It is a vital ingredient for continued unity. In this book, care is taken to encourage universal toleration by refraining from gendering God (along with other sexist references). This is not intended as disrespect to those who are used to thinking of God as "The Father." Even for those who are committed to a male concept of God, it may be helpful to reexamine these beliefs, especially if their physical fathers happened to be alcoholics or addicts.

Experience has shown, too, that if sectarian religion is allowed to interfere with each member's right to the free exercise of conscience in building and maintaining a relationship with a Higher (or Inner) Power, 12-Step fellowships often lose their effectiveness. Religious study groups may choose to study the Steps, of course, but this does not make them 12-Step programs. Traditionally, all 12-Step programs are free of affiliation with religions or other organizations. By so doing, 12-Step programs support and cooperate with all forms of belief, organized or otherwise.

As a final note, please remember to give yourself permission to enjoy your progress through the Steps on your journey to sanity and serenity. Working the Steps needn't be drudgery. Even the pain and the grief we experience in the process are the pain and grief of healing, not the old pain of continued injury we have experienced in the past. Becoming a whole person is hard work, but it isn't wasted or doomed to failure. Old fears that our best isn't good enough are echoes from the cave of darkness where disease was in control. In recovery, willingness is enough, though it often requires taking risks. Give yourself permission to risk the Steps. Give yourself permission to experience your own freedom.

STEP ONE

We admit we are powerless over (alcoholism) (other people) (a compulsive pattern), and our lives have become unmanageable.

With all the earnestness at our command, we beg of you to be fearless and thorough from the very start. Some of us have tried to hold on to our old ideas and the result was nil until we let go absolutely.

—Alcoholics Anonymous

It can be said that the pain of the Inner Child brings us to recovery, regardless of what program or addiction is involved. We come to recovery when our coping mechanisms and defenses fail. When this happens, we find ourselves face to face with our suffering, lost, frightened inner self.

It makes no difference whether this child screams because of the poisoning sustained by alcohol or drug abuse, or from the heartbreak and dread associated with unworkable relationships. The Inner Child calls out and makes us hear. Under the spur of grief, pain, and perhaps terror, we are forced, for at least a little while, out of the habitual denial that has become a mask we have worn to hide from ourselves.

Step 1 introduces us to practices of self-honesty that help us build from this flash of insight. It shows us a practical approach for nurturing and supporting our authentic self, free of compulsion and denial. The 12 Steps offer us a path to safety if we are willing to accept it.

Ultimately, we turn out to be the best experts about ourselves. As we learn to hear the voice of the self that has been buried within us, our real needs and goals, as well as our problems, gradually become clearer to us. We come to understand that this inner spiritual guidance brings the pain that brings us to recovery. We must be willing to hear the truth that lies within ourselves. As we build an honest bond with our inner selves, accepting first the child's pain and need, we are rewarded by the creativity and inspiration that are the child's gifts. If we resist, we may cut off the warning from the self within, and quickly find ourselves slipping back into confusion. Fortunately, self-honesty can be learned. It can also be practiced. All of the 12 Steps are designed to help us develop a comfortable familiarity with habits of self-honesty and to build a deep and lasting relationship with ourselves.

Step 1 poses two important challenges, both of which require self-honesty. The first challenge is stating what we see as the problem(s) we cannot solve for ourselves:

"We admitted we were powerless over..." Then, after we have admitted our defeat which caused our Inner Child to scream for help, we are then asked to follow up with a second admission. We are asked to acknowledge that, as a result of our powerlessness over this problem, *"...our lives have become unmanageable."*

When we admit that we have a problem and have begun to attend meetings, it is often the case that we find honesty a little difficult to get used to. When we begin to open our inner selves, many of us find ourselves flooded with intense and sometimes unfamiliar feelings. Forgotten memories may return. Other people's stories may stir up deep feelings in us. We may feel overwhelmed.

It is wise to anticipate that at first we may need to give over some time to simply grieving. There is a store of sad memories we may find locked away inside ourselves. Several weeks or even months may be needed to give buried feelings a chance to rise to the surface. This is not wasted time. We are giving ourselves permission to feel what we feel. This is self-honesty in action. When we do this, we begin to see our life story in a new and clearer light. Then, when we are ready to move on, we have the tools we need to heal these old wounds.

The first great truth of Step 1 is that we cannot recover from problems that we don't own and acknowledge. The definition of a problem in Step 1 is whatever we find that we are powerless to eliminate or to change by our own unaided effort and will. Addictions, compulsions, and codependencies fall within this definition. Each involves behaviors we acknowledge as harmful or undesirable but cannot resist repeating. Uncovering our problems in Step 1 is the starting point of a personal program of recovery for every member of every 12-Step program.

Step 1 asks us to accept responsibility for our present situation, no matter what circumstances outside our control may have caused the problem in the first place. Real tragedy is often a fact in our past. We don't minimize the sadness or outrage we may feel, nor do we gloss over the facts. We acknowledge that we may have been wronged in the past but take responsibility for ourselves now. We needn't carry the burden of these old wrongs into our future. We are free to own the dysfunction that has taken root in us, acknowledge that we are powerless over these patterns, and then work the Steps of recovery for ourselves. Taking this initiative in healing our hearts and minds and twisted lives is the beginning of the reparenting that takes place in recovery.

In the A.A. book *Twelve Steps & Twelve Traditions*, Bill W. noted that distortions of what begin as normal, healthy drives "cause practically all the trouble" in our lives and relationships. Out-of-balance drives for physical and emotional security (survival and commitment), for sex (gratification), and for social recognition (identity) can be seen as underlying a wide range of addictive and compulsive patterns.

Codependents mirror and react to these dysfunctions, developing coping mechanisms that become deeply ingrained, too. Codependents often can describe in detail the addiction or compulsion they are tied to by their reactions. They may also deeply dislike the problem and wish that it would go away. But until codependents detach themselves from their problem by changing their attitudes, the addiction remains. The reactions of codependents are attempts to satisfy their own deep needs for security, love, and recognition.

Chemical Abuse includes addiction to alcohol, drugs, food, and other related addictions to substance. Escape is at the core of physical addictions, which is a perversion of our instinct to bond and form commitments.

Chemical Co-Dependency is characterized by an obsession with control, manipulation, or rescuing others. This sort of behavior is also a perversion of the instinct for commitment.

Power Addictions include a range of obsessive patterns designed to keep up some sort of public front and hold on to social standing. Lack of a real sense of identity underlies this addiction.

Co-Dependent Self-Isolation develops from living with those who compulsively keep up a front at all costs. Finding fault and looking for the lie becomes compulsive, too. This sort of behavior also underlies a lack of a clear personal identity.

Compulsive Violence Disorders include all the patterns where anger is used to dominate and survive. Feeling physically threatened is the instinctive motivator.

Battered Child Co-Dependency results from living in family or social systems which run on threats of anger or violence. Deep fears for physical survival result, which, untreated, can be so overwhelming under stress that most problem solving is impossible to carry out.

Emotional Abuse Disorders include all forms of compulsively using others to gain personal gratification. Shame-based feelings about the role of sex or about having sex needs result in dishonesty and acting-out behaviors.

Emotional Co-Dependency is also based on shame concerning sex and sexual boundaries. Loss of self in relationships, fantasies about being abandoned (or rescued), and obsessions with seeking approval indicate issues in this area. Sometimes these may be buried, with only vague or fragmentary memories surfacing, at least at first.

No matter what issue or issues we find within ourselves, acknowledging these limitations is the first step in overcoming them. Whether we see our problems as addictions or among the forms of codependency, Step 1 asks us to own up. It is by admitting what our problems are that we declare ourselves in the program. No one can make this admission for us. The diagnosis of experts, pronouncements by family, employers, even the judgments of a court of law do not count, when it comes to taking Step 1.

Just as no one can force us to take Step 1 or do it for us, no one can prevent us from taking Step 1. We take this Step for ourselves and only by our own choice. This is one of the great freedoms in recovery. When we accept this fact of self-responsibility, we begin to set realistic personal limits and boundaries in what we expect from others. Such boundaries tend to free us from other people's actions or attitudes. For those who may have lived their lives in rebellion or in reaction to the impositions of others, working Step 1 may be one of the first self-directed experiences in memory.

Honesty in admitting the truth about ourselves and our situation is called coming out of denial or "surrender." Surrender in a 12-Step program is very different from the personal despair or self-denigration we have experienced in the past. Instead of opening ourselves to injury, punishment, or potential loss at the hands of other people, in coming out of denial in Step 1 we are opening ourselves to healthy change.

When we admit in Step 1 that we cannot solve or eliminate an addictive, compulsive, or codependent pattern by our own unaided efforts, we are merely ceasing to fight a battle which was already hopeless. We release ourselves from further vain attempts at control followed by heartbreaking disappointment when we give ourselves permission to admit the truth about our situation.

Of course, it may not be completely clear to us where self-control ends and addiction/compulsion/codependency takes over. We may not be certain how we have been impacted by family dysfunction. We may not know to what extent we are, ourselves, compulsive. These questions deserve serious consideration. Are we addicted to behaviors that are a threat to ourselves and others? We can also consider the self-defeating ways in which we react. Do we have bad habits, compulsions, and addictions acquired in living reactively? We catalogue all of our reactive and acting-out behaviors, whether or not we feel certain we are powerless over them.

Some issues seem more or less objective—food, drug, or other substance abuses, for example. Other issues are more subjective—such as being stuck in painful attitudes or emotions. For those behaviors which we feel we may be able to master by willpower or self-knowledge, we resolve to commit ourselves to an honest experiment. We simply test ourselves, using willpower or intellect to regain control, and note what happens. If we are able to regain control, we congratulate ourselves. If we find that we cannot, we admit that we are, indeed, powerless. This sort of self-diagnosis is at the heart of recovery.

The second challenge to self-honesty in Step 1 involves admitting how " ..our lives had become unmanageable" as a result of our problems. We examine the ways our dysfunctions have damaged us. What have we lost (or never had) as a result of our addictions or compulsions? In what ways are we unable to take care of ourselves and those we love? What kind of trouble do we have with authority in our

lives? This can be a painful experience. Not only is it sad-
dening to confront the concrete results of our problems, it
is also deflating. However, it's important that we not
indulge ourselves in fantasies of self-deception. To deceive
ourselves may cost us the very things we want most.

Those who grew up in homes where alcoholism or
other dysfunctions were present may have learned to give in
to pressures just to keep the peace. It may have been the way
to survive—to avoid getting hurt or screamed at. For those
who are the codependent children of dysfunctional families,
it can sometimes be easier to identify the ways their lives are
out of control than it is to identify specific problems. Coping
behaviors rooted in dysfunctional families may be making
our lives unmanageable. We may, for instance, still feel afraid
to stand up for ourselves. We may dread being criticized or
appearing foolish. To protect ourselves from the terror and
risk of standing alone, we may have developed the habit of
settling for what we can get, when it comes to friends or
lovers. We may allow ourselves to get involved with people
we don't respect. We may compulsively put up a front in
order to be accepted by people, socially or sexually, and then
lose respect for them when they are deceived. We may also
feel most comfortable and attracted to people who continue
to pressure and push us (like the members of our family).
Much as we may dislike being pushed, it's what we're used to
dealing with. Whether or not we can spell out an addictive
pattern in ourselves, we review the ways our lives continue to
be unsatisfying due to our involvement with others. We get
as specific as possible about the patterns we act out and
repeat. After we've located (or approximated) the patterns

we seem stuck in we note the addictions and codependencies that are involved.

Backward as this approach to Step 1 may seem—going from admitting what is unmanageable to discovering what we are powerless to change—it can be helpful in uncovering unsuspected areas of addiction or of codependence within ourselves. This may be especially true in those cases where early childhood memories are repressed. If we feel an issue may apply to us, we can trust our feelings to guide us into an honest evaluation, even if we remember little or nothing.

Step 1 is often a starting point to be used again and again as our recovery carries us forward. Whether we first come to a 12-Step program as a substance abuser, as a codependent, or as the child of a dysfunctional family, the 12 Steps of recovery provide hope if we are willing to be honest. If additional, perhaps unsuspected, issues surface as we progress, we can always come back to Step 1 to expand our horizons for recovery as we go along.

Questions to Ponder

1. Are there any circumstances or people which you have been struggling with and not getting anywhere?

2. Are there behaviors you feel powerless over, whether or not you see them as effects of alcoholism?

3. Is your life unmanageable, because you can't seem to stay out of certain patterns, ruts, fear-or-rage reactions? Describe these, including how you feel about yourself as the result of these patterns.

STEP TWO

We come to believe that a Power greater than ourselves can restore us to sanity.

Well, at first, 'I came.' Then, after I stayed "dry" a while, 'I came to.' Finally, 'I came to believe...' after I had gotten willing to give the Steps a try and really tried to work them.

—Les, an A.A. "old timer," Santa Cruz, CA

We may have perceived a sudden recognition of our personal dilemma in Step 1. Perhaps we experienced feeling overwhelmed by our powerlessness? We may even have experienced a terrifying feeling of panic, sensing that we have truly lost control of our life and our fate. We may have wished that denial would wash over us again and wrap us in a sleepy forgetfulness. At the same time, we realize that the old game just won't work for us today. If we find ourselves in such a moment of vulnerability, we have come to Step 2.

What can we believe in? Is there help? In Step 2, we are asked to open up our hearts and minds and to explore the options available to us in search of "a power greater than ourselves" who is willing and able to "restore us to sanity." Thus, we acknowledge that having "a life [which] has become unmanageable" is not a sane state of affairs.

We may not feel very confident that there is such a power, or that we can be restored to sanity by it. If we have doubt and suspicion about spiritual reality, or if we doubt that we are worthy of being helped, it can be a good practice to start gradually in Step 2. In "a power greater than ourselves," remember, we are just seeking a resource which is not powerless over whatever we admit we are helpless to overcome without help.

We are free to conceive of this power as the God or Spirit of our understanding, or as something more tangible. The 12-Step group, for instance, or the 12 Steps themselves, may be seen as "a power greater than ourselves." In the sense that the group and the Steps help people who admit having problems, this is true.

In Step 2, we are asked to try to conceive of a power, however vaguely, that could help us overcome the problems we have acknowledged in Step 1. We entertain the possibility that something can actually help us. We can do this experimentally, by the "try it and see what happens" approach. It's important only that we make a beginning and offer ourselves new options beyond denial and rationalization.

It's a good idea to itemize the "powers greater than ourselves" which may have let us down in the past. This is a practice which helps us to overcome resistances to Step 2 that are centered in unexpressed grief. Often, we feel anger, shame, or sadness as we admit the ways we have looked for help—for understanding, relief, security—and failed to find it in the past. These attempts may have lowered our self-esteem and contributed to the loss of our inner sense of identity.

Failed or inadequate "powers greater than ourselves" come in many forms. We may have been super responsible for a time, hoping to please the God of our understanding. We may have tried to earn God's help or tried to make deals with God. Either way, we may have felt abandoned, rejected, or even tricked. Now, we may be deeply angry at God or at our church, or at those people who represented religion to us in the past. We may feel we have already taken Step 2 and been let down. Perhaps we abused substances as "a power greater than ourselves." Alcohol, drugs, or food may have given us a way to turn off painful emotions, or gain feelings of courage, confidence, or happiness. Work, sex, or exercise can also be used to drown uncomfortable feelings. We may have made gods out of other people—parents, lovers, therapists—to try to find emotional relief from our inner turmoil.

When we think of the ways we have felt betrayed, do we remember any bitter promises we made to ourselves? Have we, for instance, sworn not to be fooled again? Have we resolved to keep up defenses, to not trust, not risk opening up to the possibility of disappointment? Perhaps we may find we are grimly committed to going it alone, unwilling to try Step 2.

If we had family members who abused or neglected us, we may feel even more suspicious. To children, parents are, in a real sense, powers greater than themselves. If we could not trust them, it is possible that we internalized feelings of unworthiness or a sense of being helpless pawns of fate. We may suspect any possible Higher Power as being a likely source of genuine abuse. We may feel compelled to test or defy authority when we encounter it. Suspicions rooted in the fears associated with experiences in violent families or communities can be powerful and persistent.

Fortunately, Step 2 does not ask us to *already believe* in a Higher Power that will somehow restore our lives to manageability. Instead, Step 2 starts out by saying, "We came to believe…" Remember that we are asked only to explore possible resources that we feel may work for us and then note the results. We do this just as if we were engaged in a scientific experiment. We will gradually discover what works for us. Those of us who started out as skeptics, rebels, or appeasers are not asked to deny our feelings or our opinions. We are asked only to experiment with concepts of a "power greater than ourselves" that we are willing to give an honest chance to help us, and to see for ourselves whether or not we are restored to sanity.

Some individuals find it difficult to accept the idea that some of their behaviors or attitudes have been not truly sane. Guilt, shame, and grief often make it difficult to admit our own share of a family pattern, especially those reactive behaviors that are easy to rationalize. If this is a sticking point, we can go back to Step 1 and look over the ways our own behaviors have contributed to making our lives unmanageable. Have we acted out of panic, for example? Aren't these acts, as well as any decisions made in anger, usually overreactions that serve to stir the muddy water in our lives? Do we risk blindsiding ourselves if we stubbornly justify our part in such an unbalanced drama?

When we run into resistance to a Step, we can remind ourselves that recovery isn't a footrace. Thoroughness counts for more than speed. In Step 2, we start by focusing on becoming willing to open up to a "power greater than ourself." Then, we try to be honest about whether this power actually does, in practice, help restore balance to our way of life. For many of us, doing even this much may prove a big order.

We may fear that a manageable life may not really be possible, at least not for us. Will Step 2 really work for us? The only answer is to risk it and see. What we seek is a power so strong and true that it can restore joy and meaning to our lives, no matter how twisted our lives may be. We can find a power that unconditionally embraces us no matter how unworthy we may feel. We can find it within our own hearts if we work to clear away the distortions of belief that block us from this power source within.

One of the common barriers to tapping this power source comes from unexamined personal values and old family rules we take for granted. Values are the ideas that we accept and use to define reality for ourselves. They are the bedrock we stand on when we express our point of view. Internalized values are, in effect, "powers within ourselves" because we automatically judge ourselves and others by these ideas. We live by our values, whether we are aware of them or not.

When we have values that are in conflict with a concept of a loving, unifying power within ourselves, these distortions block us from experiencing this power, even if we admit we need it. Inner conflict of this sort often shows up in daily living. We feel confused, we have a hard time making decisions, or we feel torn between the beliefs and opinions of others. Unresolved, such conflicts can produce a sense of hopelessness or depression. Feeling cut off from a source of inner well-being also produces trouble in relationships with others, as we try to get the validation from others that we need to find within ourselves.

Some of our oldest, most internalized values may be the spoken or unspoken family rules that we grew up with. Dysfunctional family rules, such as not being angry or not letting feelings of disappointment, sadness, or other "unacceptable" feelings show, may be impossible to live by with honesty. We may have been taught to value keeping up a front, sacrificing truth in the interest of protecting family secrets. We may have learned to value lying to appease someone or avoid their rage. This sort of dishonesty creates disunifying inner conflict which generates a barrier to Step 2.

If we had come to believe we had to live a lie, we may find it hard to trust others. We lose touch with our intuitive sense of judgment—another indication of being out of touch with our inner spiritual sense. We may not be able to feel the warmth and love in the relationships we have, because we may not be able to reach those feelings in ourselves. Keeping up false appearances takes a lot of energy.

Because we tend to gravitate toward others who have internalized values similar to our own, dysfunctional family rules tend to endure and be passed along from one generation to the next. If we are trying to live by family rules that are painful, we are especially inclined to seek encouragement to keep up the effort from others who have similar beliefs. This makes us susceptible to peer pressure that tends to reproduce the same, or similar, dysfunctional patterns in our adult lives. As long as we try to hang on to family rules that cut off feelings or make us lie to protect each other, we can make little progress in seeing our lives restored to sanity.

Dysfunctional family rules are like the walls of a prison that keep us locked up. Denial keeps us from seeing these walls; we just kept running into them! When it comes to working Step 2, it's important to see where our values need to change so that we can find "a power greater than [or within] ourselves..." to guide us to a sane lifestyle. Healthy values are a "higher power" without which we simply cannot recover. If we are to be restored to sanity, we will need to contact those values we have internalized that are incompatible with sane living, and replace them with new values. When we finally realize that we are free to choose values of our own, we gain a new sense of independence. Fear or rebellion against authority tends to be replaced by healthy curiosity and interest in hearing different viewpoints.

We don't lose our personal independence by seeking a "power greater than ourselves" in Step 2. Instead, we begin to develop a healthy sense of self-identity as we begin the practice of really thinking for ourselves. True independence can be seen as the personal freedom to make choices in life, combined with the necessary information and the spiritual health we need to make these choices wisely.

Questions to Ponder

1. What Power (if any) do you trust?

2. Is there a hopeless feeling or an empty, confused feeling when you ask yourself this question?

3. What resources or authorities have proved to be unreliable or inadequate sources of help in your past?

4. Does the idea of calling yourself insane frighten you or make you angry?

STEP THREE

We make a decision to turn our will and our life over to the care of God as we understand God.

...in ancient times material progress was painfully slow. The spirit of modern scientific inquiry, research and invention was almost unknown. In the realm of the material, [people's] minds were fettered by superstition, tradition, and all sorts of fixed ideas....We asked ourselves this: Are not some of us just as biased and unreasonable about the realm of the spirit as were the ancients about the realm of the material?

—Alcoholics Anonymous

Step 3 offers us the opportunity to recognize whatever form of spiritual guidance and support we are willing to accept. We have the right to define this power in any way we find acceptable. By acknowledging our relationship to an inner source of power and direction, we own that resource for ourselves. The practice of owning our choices is a way we build a clearer sense of identity.

We can call our spiritual resource by any name or no name. We are free to worship and create ceremonies of appreciation and respect in ways we find effective and satisfying. If the word "God" runs against our grain, we can modify the way we conceive of "God" to make it more comfortable and easier to embrace. We may think of this power as Spirit, nature, the Life Force, the collective unconscious—whatever we find within our own hearts. No one dictates to us or sits in judgment over our choice! It's entirely up to us. This is one of the great freedoms of the 12-Step programs.

In working Step 1, we already admitted that we have at least one problem that we can't solve or escape from by our own unaided willpower. Then, in Step 2, we explored some options for "a power greater than ourselves" that might help us, experimenting until we found a higher or inner power that we could accept and that was effective in showing us a path toward sane living. In Step 3, we are simply asked to drop our defenses and let this power help us. Much as taking Step 3 may make perfect sense, most 12-Step members find that it isn't easy to accomplish. Many 12-Step program members will admit to having trouble taking Step 3 or in sticking with the decision.

For a lot of us, Step 3 can present a mix of spiritual hurdles to be crossed, along with mental and emotional puzzles to be solved. We may need to reparent ourselves with patience, persistence, and a little humor to become comfortable with this Step.

If it's so much trouble, some will ask, why not skip over Step 3 and go on with the rest of the program? Or, why not use the group as a power greater than ourselves and leave it at that? Why make such a fuss over whether or not we have a personal spiritual connection?

The simple answer is that most of us have found that we need a personal spiritual connection in order to work the rest of the Steps effectively. Buried pain, rage, and fear we may uncover within ourselves can be overwhelming, and reliance upon exclusively human forms of support may not be adequate, or sufficiently dependable to see us through. (People have an uncanny way of going on vacation or being preoccupied with their own issues when we depend upon them instead of on our own internal resources.)

When we need an energy boost—encouragement, peace of mind, hope, and strength to see us through a challenge—we may be offered a lot of support from outside sources (meetings, books and tapes, or people in the fellowship). But this support still has to connect with a receptive place within ourselves or we simply can't be helped. In taking Step 3, we are mainly acknowledging the existence of this inner personal connection that hears truth when it is offered to us, that feels good will, and that is ours alone. We must take responsibility for ourselves in all aspects of our recovery, and that includes nurturing the receptive place within us, the connection that can receive healing and that will begin to respond joyously to life. Without this personal contact, most of us flounder and make little progress.

To begin jumping the hurdles and unraveling the puzzles of Step 3, it may be helpful to examine Step 3 concept by concept, noticing where we are resisting the Step or where we are confused about how to do the action involved in the Step. The first of these concepts involves decision making. It turns out that many of us seem to fear (or are reluctant to make) decisions. Resistance to decision making may be justified in several ways. After all, there's always the possibility of making a mistake. Or, whenever we decide to stand up for something, we run a risk of conflicting with people who disagree with us, or else feeling our own conflicted feelings.

Perhaps in the past we may have felt that we became targets when we tried to define ourselves by setting goals or limits. We may find that we never learned how to make and stick with decisions. We never learned to reap the benefits to be gained in terms of self-identity and self-respect. We may come from backgrounds where nobody made decisions, but, instead, just drifted along from crisis to crisis. Maybe we were the responsible child who was imposed upon and made to hold up under responsibilities that we were tricked or pressured into "deciding" to take on? As a result, we may now face all decisions with anxiety. We may still be in the habit of "letting others have their way," even if this means recruiting someone to make our decisions for us, even when we have the opportunity to act freely and are under no pressure to do otherwise. It's possible that the whole question of decision making may need to be reworked to reduce this hurdle to a manageable leap.

The next concept to be considered in Step 3 is releasing personal control. This release is a necessary stage in becoming receptive to guidance or direction. Many of us are more than a little reluctant to lose control. We may not welcome the prospect of turning our will and our life over to anything or anyone. Those of us who lack a clearly defined sense of self-identity can be especially troubled by such fears. We may see ourselves only in terms of what we do, our position in the community, or in our peer group. We may be so used to controlling situations or other people that we don't know who we'd be if we were to stop.

Loss of control may bring back memories and feelings of being helpless victims in families where violence threatened everyone. We may have learned to go to extremes of self-control in such families. We may be master acrobats of control, used to doing an elaborate interpersonal balancing act in order to protect ourselves or others whom we loved.

Violence or harsh competition in our communities may have been the source of training that taught us never to give up control, or to grab it back again, as quickly as we can, when we sense it's been snatched away. Many of us find that, even if we've mastered decision making, we may still be inclined to revert to old habits of snatching back control under stressful circumstances that bring up painful reminders from the past. We may find that we simply do not know how to turn it over, even when we decide we want to do so.

We need not remain passive when it comes to working this portion of Step 3. We have resources at our disposal we can use in order to become more receptive while, at the same time, strengthening our sense of integrity. Giving ourselves permission to recontact and to grieve the painful incidents which made us so addicted to self-reliance is a positive choice open to us. We can reparent the battered inner child we find in these memories. Using visualization and other creative techniques, we can bond with and rescue that child. These are the forms of nurturing we can lavish on ourselves to heal deep wounds that may be blocking us from our own inner resources. These practices help us build willingness.

Even if we are already willing to let go, practice still remains a key to success. These simple techniques—like remembering to take a deep breath and learning to ground ourselves by breathing deeply and slowly into the body's natural balance-center (located just below the rib-cage)—under stressful conditions are good practices that are easy to remember. Another good habit is remembering to say the Serenity Prayer several times a day. Making a habit to start the day with a few minutes of inspirational reading and reflection is time very well spent. A lot of 12-Step program members make a regular practice of reading one of the "a day at a time" books. A large selection of "a day at a time" reading (and tapes) can be found in most bookstores. It can be helpful to review the first three Steps every day, as a way to remind ourselves why we are in recovery and welcome spiritual power into our lives.

All of these practices build our inner connection. We join our conscious will with the spirit of Step 3 when we work to build these new habits in ourselves. New, healthy habits can be cultivated, and this includes the habit of turning it over! The key is keeping at it.

In order to feel really safe and welcome in this practice, we need to develop an unclouded sense of an inner spiritual connection that is ours to keep. Just as we are shown how to feed and dress ourselves and are taught to speak the language of our parents, we also learn much of what to think and feel about God or Spirit from our parents or from those who filled parental roles for us in childhood.

Traditionally, in healthy family systems, parents and elders in the community are there to teach us ways to recognize this spiritual contact. They demonstrate it in their own successful living. Alcoholism, drug abuse, sexual abuse, and physical violence, however, are forms of disease. When these are present, they infect family systems with fear, grief, and anger, while, at the same time, they corrode the family's basis for trust, hope, and love. In dysfunctional families there may be no elders to trust or respect whom we can turn to for guidance. Those we love the most may be victims—lacking the spiritual power and direction to save themselves or us!

Under these conditions, we may need to revamp our concept of God or Spirit in Step 3. We need a perception of God we can trust with our very lives. One of the tasks we may face is reparenting ourselves as beings with certain very real spiritual rights. Before proceeding further in Step 3, it's a good idea to think over what it means to be spiritually centered.

Being spiritually grounded means having a sense of spiritual identity in a world where we have a place as a valued human being who has a right to be alive. We're not afraid that things might fall apart at any moment. We don't feel worthless or condemned. We feel we are a part of life.

Secondly, being spiritually grounded means feeling inwardly secure—within our family, with friends, at school or work, and in the community. We are able to trust our relationships to the care of our Higher Power, even under stress. We feel ourselves to be accepted—a spiritual being among other spiritual beings. We can ask for help or companionship, but we're not overly dependent. We can enjoy our own company and time by ourselves.

Finally, being able to draw upon a spiritual contact gives us power. We find the strength and confidence necessary to risk doing our best, out of self-respect and self-appreciation. We sense the joy that comes from realizing that no one else can do our part in life, and that no one can replace us. We can also draw upon this contact for the power we need each day to overcome addictions, to face the tough decisions in life, and to heal. Mistakes we make and injuries we suffer become the images, the vivid mural painted on the wall of the days and years we are alive. It's easy to see that having a sense of spiritual wholeness has a lot to do with living life as a strong, happy, and successful person.

Claiming these basic spiritual rights can be hard work. We may feel sad or ashamed when we compare these ideals to the ways we have learned to think and feel about ourselves and God. Fortunately, though, we aren't condemned to be lost or hopeless as a result of what we learned (or didn't learn) in the past. In recovery, we can learn to reparent our spiritual Child within, and to claim as much of the ideal as we are willing to accept.

If we were taught (or shown, by the way our parents acted) that "God" was mean, condemning or cruel, or that He didn't care about us enough to make a difference in our lives, we are free to toss that old idea right out on its ear! If "God" was a word without any meaning for us, we are also free to open up our minds to new ideas—read books, listen to tapes, explore religions—seeking a personal direction we can sense in our heart.

But can we accept this good, as something we deserve? A lot of us can't—or won't—at first. Often, there's anger in the way. It's okay to express anger or sadness or disappointment—even if it's directed at an idea of "God" we feel has let us (or our family) down. If it feels more respectful, we might try thinking of anger at God as anger directed at an "old idea" about God. Twisted ideas about God account for a lot of suffering. In dysfunctional families many hurtful behaviors may have been tolerated as God's Will or "forgiven" instead of stopped. But the spiritual truth that we find in recovery does not ask us to tolerate abuse. Before deciding to turn your life and your will over to your understanding of God, try going back and checking the three ways that a healthy spiritual contact shows up in daily living. Ask yourself: Does this understanding of God give me a good feeling about being alive? Am I willing to trust this understanding of God with the care of all of my relationships? Do I feel sure I can draw the power I need from this understanding of God to do the very best I can in life, a day at a time?

Affirmations are a good way to build a concept of God or Spirit which will give you hope, trust, and the power to live well. To enhance feelings of trust and confidence in your spiritual resources, experiment with affirmations. These are powerful but simple tools for replacing old failure messages we may have internalized with positive, life-embracing messages that build our inner bond with the spiritual. If negative self-talk about your own worthiness or ability to get well makes it hard for you to feel spiritually safe, affirmations are also a good way to replace these old "voices" with new ones. If you can, identify the voice and let yourself get in touch with any feelings or memories of sadness, anger, or shame you can remember from your past about whatever message it is abusing you with. You are free to tell old negative self-talk voices to leave the temple of your inner self.

Guided visualizations are good ways to get in touch with vague memories or feelings. Practice using affirmations to replace the harsh voices you hear in self-talk, while you are letting your imagination show you pictures of the past.

Affirmations can be especially potent when they are used to contradict and replace old tapes. Examples of old tapes include old parental messages such as: "You're no good!" or "Give up. You'll never make it!" or "It will work out for those other people, but it won't for you!" Use affirmations to create simple contradictions to these messages, such as, "I am a wonderful human being!" or "I can't lose. Everything I do is guided by the Spirit!" or "I win some and I lose some, and I cherish all of my experiences as parts of a rich life!" Then speak them (out loud) directly to yourself, especially when the self-talk is taking place. Doing this works to erase the old tapes and also adds a positive new internal message.

Step 3 is not a passive experience that just happens. It's a Step that asks us to take energetic action to find a way to open ourselves up to the power we have waiting for us within ourselves. As we become willing to allow ourselves to have the power we deserve as wonderful spiritual beings moving along an important spiritual path, we receive the resources we need. This happens one day at a time as we do our share of the work.

Questions to Ponder

1. What feelings (images or memories) come up when you read Step 3?

2. Does the prospect of making a decision seem risky or threatening?

3. Do you resist (have fears about) turning your will or your life over to the care of a Higher Power? Are there memories from childhood of feeling (or of being called) undeserving or unworthy?

4. Describe God as you understand God, today. Is this a God-concept you can trust with your life?

STEP FOUR

We make a searching and fearless moral inventory of ourselves.

It is plain that a life which includes deep resentments leads only to futility and unhappiness. To the precise extent that we permit these, do we squander the hours that might have been worthwhile.

—Alcoholics Anonymous

"Drug Of Choice"

What was my drink
my delicious addiction
that led to my oppression?
My drug of choice
I held in my hand
was a glassful of depression.

—Carol Ann F., 7/30/90, Vashon Island, WA

In working the first three Steps, we start by admitting the troublesome issues that have made our lives unlivable. We then survey the resources we can tap as sources for inner power to guide us toward sane living. Finally, we commit ourselves to opening up to the care of a spiritual resource we are inspired to accept. If we have really gotten somewhere with the first three Steps, we are able to admit to ourselves why we are in recovery. We also will have begun to feel a measure of hope that growing to live successful, joyous lives may be a realistic possibility.

Drawing upon this foundation of honesty and optimism, we now turn in Step 4 to considering those factors that have made us the unique individuals we are and have been in our lives. We do this with the view of celebrating what is unique about ourselves while at the same time we strive to become objective about our own dysfunctional behaviors and attitudes.

Ideally, then, we can approach Step 4 with an enthusiastic willingness to sort through our behaviors and attitudes with the goal of keeping what we like and (eventually) getting rid of the rest. If we are fortunate enough to have a strongly developed spiritual contact that provides us with a wellspring of serene confidence, the "fearless and thorough moral inventory" in Step 4 may feel like an opportunity to grow and to explore ourselves, rather than posing a terrifying and possibly overwhelming threat.

Many of us may not come to Step 4 as ideal examples of serenity, however. We may approach Step 4 with willingness and commitment, only to be engulfed by feelings of guilt, shame, or even of disloyalty—as though being honest with ourselves is a challenge to deeply ingrained rules which have been internalized and buried below the conscious mind. Or we may feel driven to work Step 4 without feeling either confident or serene because of remorse or guilty secrets that torment us. Internal confusion, like a blanket of fog, can make it hard to see incidents in memory clearly. We may wonder if the inventory should be postponed until a more ideal condition of having internalized the first three Steps has been attained.

When we encounter these feelings and questions within ourselves about this Step, we can remind ourselves that the reason we are doing Step 4 is to find out who we are and who we have been in our lives. If we find out that we have buried fears or other feelings that spring out when we try to look at ourselves, that is definitely something to know about who we are! Likewise, if we have no peace, but are driven, haunted, or tormented, we make progress in Step 4 when we admit these painful-but-true facts.

We needn't be at an ideal state of recovery in order to begin to make progress in any phase or Step of our recovery. If we did, few of us would have much of a chance! Perfection needn't be our goal. We can gain by taking Step 4 periodically, after cycling through the balance of the Steps and reaping the benefits of embracing the entire healing process. The spiritual side of the program, over time, tends to grow clearer and stronger. This makes it more possible to be fearless and thorough when we try to look into the deep waters of ourselves in the Inventory process.

Step 4 asks us to cultivate fearless self-acceptance. Self-acceptance is not only necessary if we are to become willing to unmask behaviors we may have justified by blaming or fearing others—it is also needed to keep us from falling into the trap of self-attack.

An honest and balanced approach to facing ourselves as we really are today is what is wanted. We seek to be thorough because half-truths, rationalizations, or too rigid points of view are all masks we wear that can hide us from ourselves. It probably won't feel comfortable admitting some of what is true about ourselves, but we must be willing to be honest anyway. The pain of coming out of denial is like the pain of undergoing physical therapy to overcome a serious injury; it's a part of the healing process. We've got to see ourselves clearly in order to heal. Glossing over the facts can lead us to repeat painful patterns in our lives and in the lives of those we love.

As we work Step 4, we are beginning a powerful process of transformation from deficiency towards self-mastery. Few undertakings have greater potential. We are eliminating mental and emotional ruts that may have immobilized us for a long time. We need to make sure we have the support we need to succeed in this important undertaking. Reading, participating at meetings, and making sure we get the diet, rest, and exercise we need are ways to take good care of ourselves while we are engaged in the stress of self-examination.

Sponsorship and interaction with others in the program who are also working the Steps are also very nurturing. Step Study meetings can be especially helpful for rounding out narrow slants of looking at ourselves or others that we may not even realize we have. Working with others isn't competitive, though. We're always free to move at our own pace.

If we don't feel ready, we are free to step back until we're able to move on again. If timidity or the tendency to lose ourself in the opinions of others are major problems for us, it is important to work with a qualified individual. This can be a sponsor, a professional therapist, a friend, or a spiritual advisor—so long as it is a person we can trust.

Remember, we don't work the Steps to meet each other's expectations. The opinions of a sponsor or others in the fellowship remain suggestions only. The sharing at Step Meetings is one of the ways we seek to offer experience, strength, and hope to each other, without attaching strings of control or manipulation. We each have a responsibility to take what we can use and leave the rest.

The question of morals may be a sticking point for some in Step 4. The dictionary tells us that morals are a code of behaviors based upon value judgments as to the right and wrong ways to behave or to relate to others. Morals by this definition are simply the limits and boundaries we each set for ourselves, clearly defining what we feel is personally okay or not okay for us to do.

Some moral codes may, additionally, include value judgments as to right and wrong ways to think or even to feel. Most religions provide moral instruction as an integral part of their teachings. Sometimes these moral codes may be quite detailed, allowing for little personal choice. Many of us may associate morals with religion, perhaps with threats of punishment or social condemnation. If the idea of morals is painfully enmeshed with a rigid religious code we have chosen to reject, it's good to note that philosophies and social systems which are not religious also provide workable moral systems we can adopt or draw from.

What is wanted in Step 4's personal inventory is a system of moral standards and personal limits which will give us the boundaries we need to live without guilt and shame. We are no more bound by old, fear-based ideas in Step 4 than we are in any of the 12 Steps!

To dispel any mental confusion or feelings of shame associated with concepts of a moral inventory, it may be helpful to write a list of all the moral values we can think of and then go back over the list to determine which of these have roots within us and which are ideas we were given.

Once we get a sense of who we are, in terms of our own real values, we can put those on a list of Current Personal Values. These limits and boundaries are among the important internalized assets we can use to assess our conduct, past and present. Rules and expectations which have been imposed upon us by others can be placed upon a list of "Other People's Values (Not My Own)." These external sources of guilt and shame are usually among the most serious of our codependent liabilities.

In developing a list of Current Personal Values as principles to live by ask yourself where you really stand, or would like to stand, on such issues as:

1. **Isolation/Intimacy:** What is your ideal vision of being in touch with others? Is marriage or committed partnership an important value for you? How about your needs for privacy? Independence? Are you comfortable in one-on-one relating, or do you prefer group or family socializing?

2. **Control/Structure:** What are your limits and boundaries? What of yourself do you want to offer to others, and which others? Are you willing to ask for what you want?

3. **Obsession/Serenity:** What are your personal standards for moderation? What are the healthy sources of joy and pleasure that you celebrate in your life?

While we are trying to gain insight into our own standards, we need to cultivate the habit of noticing, at a feeling level, how we respond or react to our own thoughts, including our value judgments. If we've been in the habit of stuffing our inner feelings, the practice of noticing our own honest responses and reactions may open up new vistas. If we try to listen to ourselves, without making judgments about our reactions, we may quickly find a stronger connection to our Inner Child. We begin to develop more mental objectivity and at the same time we become more compassionate toward ourselves. We make a good start in developing a bond of self-trust between the Inner Child self and our adult self when we begin to accept ourselves in this very direct and practical way. We begin to free ourselves, too, from the burdens of shame and guilt we have carried that are based on trying to live by other people's values.

It may take some time to tell the difference between our own true values and the standards others have imposed upon us. It may well be true, too, that we find ourselves in agreement with some or many of the values we were taught.

In the next phase of the inventory, we try to glimpse the reality of how we have coped and survived so far in life. The patterns we find in this phase of the inventory are often deeply ingrained—and deeply painful. If we were influenced by dysfunctional family patterns such as threats of rejection, ridicule, or abandonment, or by violence and financial insecurity, we may have developed powerful routines to protect ourselves or those we loved.

We now go back over the years, seeking to view ourselves as the survivors we are. We go back as far as we can remember, reviewing our lives, asking ourselves, "Who hurt us? Who are we mad at? How did we react?" If there are blank periods, we note those for future exploration. We may have coped by letting people down or by reacting defensively to what seemed to threaten us. Self-attack may also be a habitual coping behavior. We may have become our own critical parent to keep ourselves from taking on challenges.

Going back through the years, how have we coped? What were the circumstances that prompted us to go on automatic and lose the power of decision? It's okay to cry and it's okay to feel sorry about these incidents. We want to welcome whatever feelings may surface in this review of our coping and surviving behaviors, even the "bad" ones. Jealousy, rage, desires for revenge—all feelings are good feelings when it comes to working Step 4. Nothing is to be gained by lying to ourselves or screening our reactions to the past. Self-acceptance means giving ourselves permission to feel whatever we may feel.

Although we allow ourselves to get in touch with any feelings or fantasies involving figures from our pasts in Step 4, we are cautioned not to undertake action on these feelings in the reality of our lives. Steps 5 through 9 are necessary parts of the healing process that we are only beginning in Step 4. If feelings that come up are very troubling, talking with a sponsor or other trusted person who is not directly involved can help.

We probably will find, too, that we behaved or tried to behave in ways that we can now see were actually pretty healthy, assertive responses to some of the pressures we encountered. If our healthy responses were attacked or discredited, we may find that we have suppressed a great store of rage and frustration. A sense of injustice is at the root of most resentment.

In this portion of the inventory, we note whom we are angry with, the ways we were abused or made to feel inadequate, what that we needed or wanted was interfered with, and how we feel as a result.

We must be as specific as possible about these incidents. Feelings may be hard to contact, or difficult to name. It is helpful to construct a table such as the one below for this portion of the Inventory:

A Resentment Inventory

	Why?	**Affects** (Basic Needs):	**I Feel:**
Myself:	I wrote bad checks to cover expenses for food, utilities	Identity, Survival	Worthless, weak, and unable to take care of myself
My Stepparent:	Stole my share of family insurance	Survival, Commitment	Abandoned, ashamed
Siblings:	Took heirlooms for themselves and wanted me to have nothing	Identity, Gratification	Rejected, ridiculed, used, betrayed, emotionally battered

In the next phase of the Inventory process, we go back over the Table above and make an effort to get in touch with our fears. Once again we ask ourselves, in each incident, what did we fear we'd lose or fail to get? We try to describe our fear in detail.

1. Do we find we are afraid that we won't survive? That we won't be accepted or cared for? Do we fear that we may be left alone (or trapped)? Does ridicule or looking like a fool strike terror in our hearts?

2. We look for the patterns created by fear in our lives. Have we been appeasers, losing our integrity in compliance, flattery, or by presenting a false front to those who we felt had power over us in some areas of our life? Have our deep fears taken over in some situations, trapping us into reactions that trigger crises and uproar in our lives? How much has fear colored our behaviors in transactions that involve the basics, such as family, sex relations, career and money-matters?

Often, feelings of shame, embarrassment, or arrogant self-justification may prompt us to minimize or gloss over these questions. Fears seem to have a life of their own. Tracking them down is always a challenge.

If we are inclined to sidestep this phase of the Inventory, we remind ourselves that our unexamined fears usually control our behaviors, especially under stress. We may be living lives largely defined by our fears. It is by tapping "...the courage to change the things we can..." and facing up to our fears, that we begin to change our way of life.

We complete the Inventory in Step 4 by setting up a balance sheet of our personal assets and liabilities. Our balance sheet is a thumbnail sketch of what works and what needs help in our personalities, a summary we can refer to easily as we move on to the other Steps. We sort through what we have written, first noting any characteristics we admire in ourselves. We look for courage, kindness, willingness to try, a spirit of adventure—any and all characteristics we see in ourselves as worthy, valuable, or spiritual. We claim these assets, being careful not to leave out minor or "to be expected" positive qualities about ourselves.

Then, going back over all we have written, we try to be honest about what our real liabilities are. Do we tend to lie to ourselves rather than to admit to an unattractive bit of truth, for example? Do we get involved in crisis after crisis to avoid facing up to basic responsibilities? We seek to discover what the underlying weaknesses are within ourselves, not as an exercise in self-attack, but as an important step forward into new freedom. We remind ourselves that our goal is to build a starting place for self-transformation now.

Finally, we go back to our assets list and give ourselves credit for the assets we have earned by our work in doing the Inventory. We also remember to give ourselves credit for having survived and coped through the difficulties and trials of our past. We acknowledge ourselves as the unique expressions of life we each are and we thank ourselves for doing this work.

In conclusion, trying to get well in a 12-Step program without taking Step 4 is like trying to follow a treasure map without a starting place. Without first knowing where we started, we're unlikely to find the prize—no matter how carefully we follow the rest of the clues.

Recovery is a search for the personal treasure of rich, joyful living. In this treasure hunt there is no need for competition among the searchers. Instead, we help each other. Of course, we do want—and need—the treasure of addiction- and compulsion-free living. We aren't just playing a game. Still, working the Steps needn't be all hard work and pain. Among the best attitudes anyone can have for working the 12 Steps is a spirit of discovery and adventure. We need an element of fun. We also need the enthusiasm that comes from doing something exciting. One of the best testimonies of a living faith is to have the cheerful confidence to try something new and to do it with a light touch.

Instead of the old message we may have heard—that whatever is valuable is very hard, maybe impossible—we seek to get the message in the 12-Step program that the good things in life are attainable. We can cultivate the spirit of adventure to see us through the rough spots. Once we've established this attitude, we can use it on anything else we take on in life that's new or challenging.

Questions to Ponder

1. Can you feel your feelings, identify them, name them for what they represent?

2. Is there something that is a "guilty secret" in your past—crimes, sex behavior?

3. Do you have secret fantasies of love or revenge?

4. Do some behaviors or circumstances bring up memories from childhood, even very vague ones? Describe these memories or images as completely as you can, whether or not they seem to make sense.

STEP FIVE

We admit to God, to ourselves, and to another human being the exact nature of our wrongs.

Risks

To laugh is to risk appearing the fool.
To weep is to risk appearing sentimental.
To reach out for another is to risk involvement.
To expose feelings is to risk exposing your true self.
To place your ideas, your dreams, before a crowd
is to risk their loss.
To love is to risk not being loved in return.
To live is to risk dying.
To hope is to risk despair.
To try is to risk failure.
But risks must be taken, because the greatest hazard in life is
to risk nothing.
The person who risks nothing, does nothing,
has nothing and is nothing.
They say they avoid suffering and sorrow,
but they cannot learn,
feel, change, grow, love, live...
Chained by their attitudes, they are slaves.
They have forfeited their freedom.
Only a person who risks is free.

—Anonymous,
Submitted by Dave L., Fortuna, CA, & Joan N., Chicago.

In considering Step 5, we confront our vulnerabilities. We risk the possibility of personal rejection, ridicule, public exposure. To individuals who may have avoided intimacy, dreaded criticism, and distrusted authority, Step 5 poses a definite challenge.

We risk stepping out of isolation. We are asked to go beyond living inside our private theories and fantasies and take action in a larger world, a world which includes a concept of God, ourselves, and at least one other human being. Breaking old habits of spiritual, personal, and social isolation and replacing these with fearless honesty is the purpose of Step 5.

Why do we take Step 5, if it asks so much of us and challenges so much self-protective armor we rely upon? The answer is that we don't take Step 5 until we've come to an inner realization that the old games, whatever they were, don't work for us anymore. If isolation were a tolerable way of life for us, most of us would not have come into a 12-Step program of recovery. If we could have lived happily with our secrets—or just gotten by in even relative comfort—most of us have to admit we probably would have done so, rather than completed Step 5.

Once, we may have successfully protected ourselves by shutting down, by shutting up, or by running away. However, these self-imposed forms of isolation no longer worked for us. Feelings—guilt, shame, self-doubt, fears (with and without names), grief, bitterness—haunted us. We could neither shut them off nor escape.

With torment so internalized, we may have felt locked in an intolerable prison of loneliness and despair. This is a feeling of spiritual isolation so terrifying we simply had to find a way to be free. We couldn't live otherwise. For most of us, the willingness to work Step 5 hinges upon remembering how isolated and alone we felt before we found the hope of recovery. We become willing to risk sharing our secrets when we realize that this is what we have to do to rejoin the human fellowship and cease being creatures apart.

If we discover that we still fear a condemning, punishing form of Higher Power, we review Steps 2 and 3. We remind ourselves that, as a recovering person who has been directed to a 12-Step program, we have already been given evidence of our Higher Power's good will. We remind ourselves that we are a part of a spiritual universe. We say the Serenity Prayer. Ultimately, we share any fears of punishment or condemnation we have about God with the God of our understanding. After all, it's just another part of telling the whole truth.

Many of us discover that we are plagued by another form of isolation: the isolation of self-loss. We may be very much in the habit of snowing ourselves. Instead of communicating with ourselves by thinking over questions that come up and forming an opinion, we may be in the habit of simply parroting old, rigid ideas. We may, in fact, tell ourselves that we feel or believe in ways that we really don't.

Why do we lie to ourselves? Maybe we feel inadequate to think for ourselves. Maybe we fear if we were to let ourselves think or feel without using a stranglehold of control, that a monster of selfish, self-will would leap out of us. Often, we are in the habit of lying to ourselves because we really don't like ourselves very well. In Step 5, hard as it may be, we are asked to treat ourselves like people we can trust.

There is another type of problem we can run into when it comes to telling ourselves the truth in Step 5. We may have internalized some coping mechanisms that are entirely automatic and seemingly beyond our control. It is not unusual for people with addictive patterns to blank out under some forms of stress—pressured sexual situations, arguments about money, or responsibilities or situations where there is fear of physical violence. Inability to feel feelings or to think clearly are not unusual reactions to stress. When, in Step 5, we are faced with sharing secrets about ourselves, these ingrained coping mechanisms may crop up, even when we are committed to honesty. We may get foggy or forget. If we have learned to protect ourselves by automatically shutting down under certain pressures, what can be done about it?

The A.A. "Big Book" states (chillingly) on page 58, "...Those who do not recover are people who cannot or will not completely give themselves to this simple program, usually men and women who are constitutionally incapable of being honest with themselves. There are such unfortunates....They are naturally incapable of grasping and developing a manner of living which demands rigorous honesty. Their chances are less than average."

If we fear that we are among the unfortunates so cut off from ourselves as to be incapable of self-honesty, what can we do to improve our chances for recovery? Fortunately, there are many reparenting techniques we can apply to help us renegotiate even our deeply internalized coping mechanisms, if we are willing to do the work. Often, very early incidents which prompted reactions of rage, shame, and grief in us are at the root of persistent fogginess or automatic shutdowns. If we will do the work, the Inner Child is always capable of self-honesty.

We may need to re-explore incidents from the 4th Step Inventory that were confusing, or that prompted rage or revulsion, utilizing Inner Child techniques. Shame and anger may also be trapped in our bodies—in chronically stiff joints or muscles. Body work, massage, or movement work may also be very helpful tools for getting out of self-isolation.

Many of us may be inclined to skip over this aspect of coming out of self-isolation in Step 5. We may say that these innovative techniques aren't for us—that they have nothing to do with the simple business of telling the truth. We may be so used to relying on the rational, thinking side of ourselves that we are entirely distrustful of the prospect of opening up to the feeling side. Perhaps we think of our Inner Child as just a sniveler, a weak crybaby we want to leave behind. Denial, rigid ideas, and pride are all barriers to self-honesty that can keep us locked in self-isolation. If we will take the time in working Step 5 to improve communication with our creative self, we can only gain as our capacity for self-honesty increases and we become more able to accept ourselves.

When we consider disclosing our secrets to someone else it's not unusual to experience a rush of defiance. We may be bitterly humiliated by memories of incidents where our confidences were abused. Waves of distrust, fear of rejection, of ridicule, or of punishment may stir up a great deal of resistance.

In the face of these reactions, it may seem impossible to go further. Some feel so exposed at the prospect of taking this portion of Step 5 that they think of quitting the 12-Step program entirely—either to go back to the old lifestyle or to take up an alternative that eliminates or delays disclosure. Unwillingness to trust or to risk confiding in another human being may be a way of life for us. Social isolation can be a powerful habit. It may not yield easily to change.

We are thus faced with an objective barrier to continued recovery. We begin to realize that these issues of defiance and fear simply are not going to evaporate by themselves. At this stage of recovery, social isolation is not something imposed upon us by others. It's a condition we have internalized. Action is required to free ourselves. As with most kinds of objective problems, practical solutions are in order. Here are some practical strategies to overcome resistance to Step 5.

Reaction to authority is often at the root of problems of defiance or distrust. It may be helpful to go back to Step 3 and reconsider your concept of God. Ask yourself: When I say "I won't!" who am I defying? Is my concept of God or Spirit too weak or too mean to be trusted to protect me? We can afford the time to go through Step 3 again if it seems appropriate. A loving, powerful concept of God is essential to our success. Time we spend opening our hearts and minds to Spirit is never time wasted!

Using the Serenity Prayer may be helpful. We can ask that we be given serenity and courage necessary to go forward. We can ask for wisdom to choose a person who will not betray our confidence.

When we are spiritually grounded, we can set about considering whom we will share our 5th Step with. It's a good idea to put "principles before personalities" in this.

Confidentiality is vital. Gossip is to be avoided. A good friend on a lunch date may not be right for the 5th Step. We owe it to ourselves to be thoughtful in selecting a person who understands the basics of the 12-Step process and will respect our trust.

A majority of 12-Step program members share their 5th Step with a sponsor. This is usually someone they have come to trust over a period of weeks or months in a relationship centered on working the program. Others may choose to share with someone outside the 12-Step program—a counselor, a priest or minister. It is usually not a good idea to share these confidences with a family member, spouse, or lover who may be directly impacted or burdened by what is shared. Doing this may add more pain and confusion than it eliminates.

For a thorough Step 5, we will want to arrange sufficient time without interruptions. Feedback is important. Several hours—an afternoon or evening—free of ordinary distractions is in order. If you are working with someone who cannot give you such a chunk of time, or if your own schedule won't allow it, be realistic. Plan, discuss, and commit to a sufficient number of meetings to get through all of Step 5 without rushing. Don't short yourself. If the person you have asked to work with you is unable to give you enough time to do a thorough 5th Step, it may be wise to find someone else instead of minimizing the project.

There is one more step in overcoming social isolation in Step 5: Don't put it off! Acting in new ways, even when we are convinced that these new ways are healthy, can feel pretty uncomfortable. Coming out of isolation requires courage.

We need to guard against any tendency we have to say we aren't ready when what we mean is that we aren't willing.

Probably nothing does more for self-esteem than acting on convictions. Many feel that in taking Step 5 we change. When we take the action that Step 5 asks of us, we are demonstrating our ability to act with real courage. Our faith ceases to be hypothetical. We are living it. For many of us, this is a very great change.

Sometimes, there is a question of what to share. Some of our wrongs are easier to grasp than others. It's a fairly straightforward matter, for instance, to admit that we have robbed a filling station (if we have) or to admit that we've cheated on a spouse or partner. Nothing is to be gained by concealing any dark secrets in Step 5. Those who have tried to leave some things buried usually discover they have simply continued to bury themselves.

Neither is it advisable to work Step 5 with someone who you feel will censure you for aspects of your chosen lifestyle—such as sexual preferences—so that you are tempted to conceal some aspects of yourself. Step 5 is not something we undertake to expose ourselves to unexamined judgments and fears of others. It's important to be certain—before beginning the sharing that takes place in Step 5—that the person we will be working with accepts us.

In addition to specific incidents, it is important to look at the wrongs caused by patterned behaviors. Do the incidents we feel shame and remorse about follow a pattern? If we have robbed a filling station, have we also stolen money (or goods) from friends, family? Do we feel so unworthy deep inside that we live out a pattern in which our basic survival depends upon sneaking and stealing? Are we locked in a pattern of envy or stealing to get even or to put up a front? These issues also must be discussed.

When we talk these matters over with a trusted person, we often are in for a surprise. Rather than the judgment and criticism we may have feared, we may find compassion and a sense of humor, which will help what we may have feared would be a pretty gloomy undertaking. The sponsor will probably ask that we explore our underlying motives. For most of us, these deeper patterns are what have made our lives unhappy and unsuccessful.

Most of us find Step 5 to be a miracle as well as a surprise. More than just social acceptance seems to flow into our lives when we have worked Step 5. Even concerns we may have brooded over for a long, long time may be affected in ways we could not have imagined in advance. It is not important that we have a sense of faith in advance to use Step 5 effectively. Just taking the action and telling the truth seems to be enough. No longer isolated outsiders in life, we find our fear of others and of economic insecurity tending to evaporate. Once we have begun, most of us find that we gradually enter a new world of hope and transformation.

Exposing ourselves to abuse or punishment is not the purpose of Step 5. In this Step, we don't fight off our anxieties about exposure, or ridicule ourselves for being fearful. Instead, we find ways to do what it takes to get the support we need to go forward.

It may be that one of our problems is a tendency to expose ourselves to abuse. Some of us may have learned to be our own worst enemy. If we have completed an inventory and have admitted incidents that we are ashamed about, we still should not jump to conclusions about what we have to do until we have talked things over with a person we can really trust. Even if we feel certain that "we know what they will say," Step 5 asks us to risk checking out what at least one other person does say, when we talk to them. We are asked to do this to get out of living in our heads.

Taking Step 5 isn't like telling our secrets to a friend. The talking we do in Step 5 is a major step we take to change and heal our lives. This is very different from complaining or trying to get someone to help with a cover-up operation. One of the ways we can reparent ourselves in Step 5 is to be sure that the person we share with is thoroughly familiar with the 12 Steps and really understands the goals of Step 5.

If there are issues such as physical or sexual abuse which may be still ongoing in our lives, talking to a knowledgeable person, such as a professional counselor, is in order. Sponsors in a 12-Step program aren't meant to be substitutes for getting legal and other forms of appropriate help. We all have the right to safety and respect in our lives. This is true even though we may feel inclined to protect others or to minimize the injuries we may suffer. The power in Step 5 is lost if we insist on burying the truth about our situation, whatever it is. If we feel threatened, we owe it to ourselves to go to someone who potentially has the resources to help us out. If we will take the responsibility to go this far, it's the responsibility of a loving Higher Power to see us through to freedom.

Here are some warnings for working the 5th Step:

1. Don't share something at a meeting that would really hurt you or cause big trouble if it got out. This is true even though all 12-Step meetings have a commitment to the pledge, "What you hear here, let it stay here." 12-Step programs don't usually screen their memberships, though, so violations of this principle do sometimes happen. If in doubt, always share one-on-one with someone you respect and trust before talking in a meeting.

2. Don't share explicit details about sexual experiences at meetings, unless you are in a fellowship which focuses on sex issues. This is the sort of information that can easily be abused, especially in school, work or a small community.

3. Don't divulge anyone's name when sharing your 5th Step, either one-on-one or at meetings. Protect yourself from revenge or gossip. It is definitely okay to share the name of a person who is molesting or abusing you, but only with a knowledgeable person who is qualified to help.

With these guidelines in mind, Step 5 becomes a pathway to support. When we share, we learn. We learn that we aren't alone and that others have had similar experiences and feelings. In sharing, we find solutions. We hear what others have to say. We feel their love. Step 5 offers us a new and different way of life.

Questions to Ponder

1. What do you fear that God as you understand God won't forgive?

2. What are you ashamed or afraid to tell anyone about yourself?

3. What isn't "important enough" to bother with, or to share?

4. Who do you know accepts you just as you are?

STEP SIX

We become entirely willing to have God remove all these defects of character.

Mary had a doll she loved very much. The doll had lost an arm, so Mary asked God to fix the doll. Nothing happened, so she again asked God to please fix her doll's arm. Still nothing happened, and finally Mary cried out, "God, why haven't you fixed my dolly's arm?" God answered, "I was waiting for you to let go of her."

—Anonymous, submitted by Martha H.,
Blue Lake, CA

I've come to see that relationships are something you have, not something you are...

—Charlie T., Humboldt, CA

We may start out a little puzzled at the focus of Step 6; we may be used to thinking more in terms of problems than character defects. Isolation is a problem, for example—not a character defect. We may be sharply aware of several problems we face in life, but only dimly conscious (if at all) of our character defects.

Step 6 reminds us that we can solve problems only by becoming willing to change something about ourselves. If we are isolated, for instance, what are we doing to keep ourselves that way? We have to bring the focus to where it can do us some good—back to ourselves—if there is going to be a change.

The character defects we work to release in Step 6 are the behaviors and attitudes that keep us bound to our problems, whatever those problems may be. Since most of what we do that causes us (and others) pain we do over and over again, these character defects will generally be found among the habitual behaviors and ingrained attitudes we have. Habits are the limits we really live by, whether we're aware of them or not. Habits may account for how we spend nearly every moment of our day. Our lives may fairly dance or drag along, structured by the routines we have.

Many of our identified life problems, especially those that reoccur, are bound to us by our own habits. Many problems simply cannot go away until we become willing to let go of the thinking and acting that ties us to them. If recovery is to be a living experience and not just something we read and talk about, we're probably going to have to become willing to say goodbye to a lot of our old, habitual behaviors.

A present character defect may be a former coping behavior that once was an important part of our survival kit. But, in recovery, it becomes excess baggage. We usually aren't aware of the routines we don't need any more until they begin to cause trouble.

It is said that people don't change behaviors that work. Take, for instance, habits of appeasement or defensive touchiness which may have been lifesavers when we had to fend off threats in dysfunctional relationships. These reactions can—and usually do—hang on into recovery. We may continue to placate or to bristle in relationships and situations where no comparable threat exists. We may also continue to feel and act more vulnerable than is actually necessary. If we do this, we suffer needlessly as we negate our own power in situations where a more positive role is possible for us.

Step 6 is another action Step. The first action in Step 6 is review. If we have done the Steps that lead up to Step 6, we will have made a written Inventory in Step 4 of issues that brought us to recovery. This is a good place to start. Now we look at our inventories again to see, as well as we can, how the issues we have pinpointed as troublesome still hang on and have power in our lives. Are we strengthening the values we found in ourselves by our present habits? Or do our habits undercut our vision for the future?

It's a good idea to continue the practice begun in Step 5 of sharing these insights with someone we trust. Honest interaction with a sponsor can be very helpful. Without rationalizing, we seek to examine our day-to-day behaviors. We want to seek out any indications that we may be dragging our old miseries, in the form of habitual reactions, into our present lives. Are we still defending ourselves from threats that were once quite real, but now are behind us? Are we objectively still being threatened or do we just feel threatened? Do we continue to act from habitual fears, habitual suspicions, or other defensive patterns? On the other hand, do we continue to expose ourselves to threats that we now know will do us harm?

In Step 6 we need to become aware of ourselves in the present. What do we actually do, think, and feel? We want to try to see ourselves in terms of all of our habits, not just the most glaring or flattering ones. From the time we open

67

our eyes in the morning until our final sleepy yawn at night, how are we living? Which side of the bed do we get up on? Which shoe goes on first? Do we eat breakfast? Meditate? Exercise?

This self-scrutiny may seem like a pretty silly idea. We may be tempted to skip part—or all—of it. We may ask, "What's this got to do with my becoming willing to have character defects removed?" Some of us may become more belligerent, feeling that this sort of inquiry is nobody's business. "What am I supposed to do—ask my sponsor if I'm brushing my teeth in a spiritual way? I did Step 5. Let God decide what my defects are."

We may feel we are too busy or that we already know how our Inventory liabilities show up as character defects in our lives. But do we? Often we may be more willing to inventory our problem behaviors in Step 4 than to actually let them go. We may be inclined to speak of our issues in general terms or to characterize them as past mistakes, as though they are no longer a part of our lives. Insight alone, however, doesn't heal compulsions or remove ingrained fears. We have to become willing to actually change and let go of our old ways in order to move closer to our inner potentials.

Why do we seem to be so attached to our old ways, even when they directly interfere with our hopes and goals? Do we have to admit finally that we are addicted to wrongdoing and are therefore morally weak? There is another way to look at it. We now know that the grief process isn't exclusively about death or separation. It's also about change.

Change in our lives—even the change that comes with victory and triumph—is commonly associated with a feeling of loss, anxiety, or sadness. We move on in life, stage by stage, day by day. Feelings of sadness or loss can come upon us with success as much as with failure. Change, especially sudden change, may bring up memories of other events which were painful or frightening. We may remember times, too, when we risked something and suffered disappointment. It's also not unusual to feel near-panic at the prospect of letting go of old defenses. We wonder what will we do, instead. We may feel we face a loss of identity if we let go of a strongly held defense. Indeed, to the extent that we've lost ourselves in codependently seeing ourselves in reaction to others, this feeling can seem very real. But we really are not these fear-based behaviors. We are the inner self these behaviors have been set up to protect. We need to ask our Higher Power to give us the willingness we need and to help us move to reclaim who we really are and can be. In Step 6, as we become willing to allow for the possibility of gradual change, we slowly move out of the reactions that have kept us anchored to the past.

It takes time to become willing to accept the feelings that come up for us when we face change. We have to give ourselves time to gradually let go of the past. But, as we give ourselves permission to feel and let go, the changes heal us and carry us forward to a brighter future free of our old ruts.

When we realize that we need not be bound by our old habits and reactions, a more positive self-image becomes possible. Limiting self-concepts such as, "That's just the way I am," can be challenged by consciously choosing to behave differently. The more we exercise the options we have to change, the greater this freedom to change becomes. Instead of a passive or defiant "That's the way I am" stance of the past, we can adopt an attitude of "This is how I choose to be today."

No matter how much a behavior may have helped us cope with the impossible in the past, does this behavior serve us now? If it doesn't, then it's up to us to become entirely willing to let it go.

We must remember that we are not in recovery to meet other people's standards—just our own. If we find that we aren't willing, today, to let go of some behaviors that we might ideally like to eliminate, self-honesty remains the best policy. We can ask our Higher Power for the willingness to change, if it is in keeping with our highest good. We can help ourselves become more willing by picturing alternatives to behaviors that remain in the way. Alternatives and the willingness to accept them will come.

If there are behaviors that we choose to keep, even though others may object to them, we are honest about this, too. Success is to be measured in terms of how well we can accept and live happily with ourselves. We want to live up to our own ideals, not other people's. With self-responsibility comes genuine independence. Codependent reliance upon the approval of others is gradually replaced by trust in the guidance we receive from our Higher Power. If we can accept ourselves and we are willing to live with the consequences of the choices we make, who's to act the judge?

We do, however, need to remind ourselves to come back to this step periodically to review our own progress. What may be useful and comfortable in our lives today may become excess baggage tomorrow. Recovery is a dynamic process of continuing change. Rather than a steep staircase we climb once, the 12 Steps are more like stepping stones that lead along a path we can follow, day by day. When we take Step 6, we have the opportunity to act, not react, as we choose to release or reaffirm behaviors. The freedom to choose is a blessing of recovery.

Questions to Ponder

1. What old behaviors that used to serve you don't work any more and are now in your way?
2. If you let them go, stopped doing them, what might happen?
3. What do you want for yourself instead of your old habits, behaviors, or attitudes?
4. Is it worth the risk to let go now?

STEP SEVEN

We humbly ask God to remove our shortcomings.

For the whole earth is a point, and how evil a nook in it is this thy dwelling....

—Emperor Marcus Aurelius,
Roman (121–180 a.d.)

Dear God,
help me turn
my stumbling blocks
into
stepping stones!

—Carol Ann F., 7/3/90, Vashon Island, WA

If we've managed to come this far in the Steps, we've learned much about ourselves. Probably we have discovered unsuspected assets in ourselves, as well as liabilities. We've started to use powerful new strategies for self-change in our lives. Now, in working Step 7, we are faced once again with the question of whether we still need a spiritual boost to see us through. Answering this question brings up the concept of humility, which is central to Step 7.

The purpose of Step 7 is not to rob us of confidence or to humiliate us as incompetent. The issue instead is one of balance. The concept of humility we are asked to cultivate in Step 7 is a genuinely positive quality, one that is potentially

of great help to us. Step 7 asks us not to overcommit ourselves by relying too much on self-reliance. When we ask
our Higher Power to remove our liabilities, we are giving
Spirit a chance to become active in our lives.

Humility allows us to look at situations realistically.
How big or small a task do we face? It also allows us to be
honest about how powerful or weak we and our resources
are in relation to that task. A professional consultant such as
an engineer is actually being humble, in the sense that we
mean it, when s/he says, "Yes, I can build that bridge. We'll
need these materials and helpers to do the job." The engineer is simply looking at the situation honestly for what it
is. S/he doesn't gloss over the difficulties or inflate them. A
competent engineer takes responsibility for knowing where
to get what's needed to complete the job.

An unqualified person might try to bluff. S/he might
underestimate the materials or fail to set up the necessary
help. The project might fail and someone might get hurt. A
bluffer deserves to lose credibility. In recovery, we are our
own trustworthy experts. Humility is a tool that we need to
cultivate so we can see our own situation clearly and realistically. We must reach our for whatever help we need to
realize our vision.

In the previous Steps, we sized up the project. We
learned to turn within, to draw upon our spiritual resources.
As we learned self-honesty and self-acceptance, we probably
began to trust ourselves, perhaps for the first time. What we
have done so far stands as a foundation for the lives that we
want to build. To the extent that we have gotten to know
ourselves—with both strengths and weaknesses—we have
learned humility as we mean it in Step 7.

Now we take a look at our liabilities and bad habits. We admit the limits of our present powers. What can we do for ourselves? Where are we stumped, powerless to change? As our own trustworthy experts, we need to know when to reach for help. If we were to try to rely on a bluff, the structure of our lives can become shaky. This is the spirit of balanced humility in which we turn to our Higher Power and ask God to remove our shortcomings.

The asking for help in Step 7 isn't hysterical pleading, nor is it a matter of giving detailed instructions to God. Just as we have done our part in taking the Steps that lead up to this one, we now are asked to trust that our Higher Power will transform us for our highest good. Just as we've become willing to "Let go..." through the exercises in Step 6, we now take a deep breath and "...Let God!" For Step 7 to be accomplished, we must actually release the shortcomings to God's care and will. The asking that occurs in Step 7 is grounded in the conviction that our Higher Power is present, available, and willing to mold our lives to our highest good.

As we grow in the inner perspective necessary for success in Step 7, we may notice a release of tensions that is directly physical, whether or not help with a physical problem is an issue with us. When we succeed in really "letting go and letting God," inevitably a burden is lifted from us. It is a good practice, for this reason, to link verbal practices of asking that our shortcoming be removed with the practice of techniques for relaxation. As we remind ourselves to associate a physical sense of relaxation with "...letting God," we can actively cultivate the healthy humility we seek within our bodies, as well as within our minds. We become more peaceful and serenely confident physically as agitation, tension, and timidity within the body is released.

Relaxation practices need not be complicated to be effective. Taking in some long, slow breaths is a simple, effective practice. Other relaxing practices include taking a warm bath, listening to music, swimming, taking an unhurried walk, or having a massage. Yoga and other disciplined approaches to relaxation are also fine ways to cultivate Step 7's harmonious release of stresses in body, mind, and spirit.

Another method for cultivating humility while building self-respect is to school ourselves to remember where we came from before we found recovery and to count the blessings we have already received. Techniques for developing an attitude of gratitude are easy to learn. If we are feeling inclined to take personal credit for all that we have accomplished since we started getting well, it may be helpful to remember how we were at our first meetings. Were we confused? Frightened or in pain? Were we insecure in some ways that were utterly unacceptable? If we hadn't come into recovery, what might have happened? What happened to help us? Did that help come from self-sufficiency?

We want to contrast how we were with how we are, today. How much of this is due to what we've learned in recovery? We own the benefits we have already received from being in a fellowship along with what we've gained from tools we've learned to use in our lives. When we count the blessings we have gained and contrast these with the pain of what might have been, not only do most of us feel grateful, but current difficulties may lose a measure of their terror and their sting.

It is humble to acknowledge the progress we have made. It isn't humble to minimize the positive change in our lives, nor is it humble to put ourselves down. These are very dysfunctional concepts of humility. They are tied to false ideas that our Higher Power wants us to humiliate ourselves, which just isn't true. When we rejoice in recovery, it's a form of praising and celebrating the presence of a living Spirit in our lives.

Questions to Ponder

1. How has recovery affected you and your life already?

2. What are some of the fruits of recovery you are experiencing now?

3. Do you feel you can trust the God of your understanding to mold your character?

4. Center yourself by breathing into your solar plexus (the area just below your diaphragm) and let go! Feel how it feels. Take another breath. Feel. Let yourself explore this experience.

STEP EIGHT

We make a list of all persons we have harmed and become willing to make amends to them all.

The pain of one is the pain of all; the honor of one is the honor of all.

—Native American proverb

As much trouble is caused in this world by taking offense as by giving offense.

—Morry S., Trinidad, CA

In Step 8, we undertake the work that heals our relationships with other people. This may sound like a very big order—and, for most of us, it is. Some of our personal relationships may have become the focus of frustration, heartbreak or confusion, perhaps for a long time. Indeed, some individuals entwined in our histories may have died or exited from our lives. Healing change may seem, at first glance, impossible.

Our purpose, however, in Step 8 is to build ourselves a gateway into a bright new world where functional relationships are possible for us. Working Step 8 is a spiritual undertaking, like all the Steps. We seek to bring a new dimension of spiritual understanding to bear in the relationships we have, or have had, so that healing becomes possible in us. Persuading other people is not the goal of Step 8, and we are careful not to take on that responsibility. We remind ourselves that, in a spiritual universe others, too, have the option to heal, if and when they are willing to accept that option. We keep the focus on clearing our side of the street, even as we reconsider the feelings and needs of those we love, and we trust the outcome of our efforts to the care of our Higher Power.

Just what do people have a right to expect from each other, anyway? In the 12-Step programs of recovery we accept ourselves as being worth healing, as the spiritual children of a Loving Parent. As worthy, valued individuals we have spiritual rights including the rights to feel secure, accepted, cared for, and appreciated. The promise of recovery is the promise of having these deep basic needs met, by the action of God as we understand God in our lives.

Just as we joyfully claim and affirm these rights for ourselves, we must, logically, affirm them for others—all others—whether we are acquainted with them or not, whether we like them or not. If any of us has the right to heal and be whole, then each of us has that same right. Human beings harm each other in direct relation to how much they ignore or lose sight of this underlying spiritual common ground.

All relationships, then, are at core spiritual connections between spiritual beings. As people with God-given value, we can expect to have our basic worthiness acknowledged in the many forms of care and support we receive and give to others. If we are tempted to deny this, we remind ourselves that, though these expectations may not always be met by others, it is still our right to have them. Self-respect and respect of others are really other names for acknowledging the God-centered nature that's within us all. In practical terms, however, unreleased anger or fear tends to cut us off from feeling our underlying connection with some individuals or groups. Nothing is to be gained by denying such blocks where they exist; the path free is the path through.

We receive practical survival-help, guidance, affection, and/or companionship from others. This starts before we are even born, or we wouldn't survive. What we do for each other ranges from a little to a lot, depending on the relationship involved. In turn, we are instruments in the lives of others. Acknowledging some degree of spiritual "common ground" is implied in every contact with others. All interactions involve honoring each other's spiritual identities.

Of course, we don't have the same degree of responsibility toward all people in our lives. Neither do all people have the same degree of responsibility toward us. Personal commitments and responsibilities depend on the kind of bonding we feel, along with other more contractual responsibilities. Parents, for example, not only usually feel deeply bonded with their children, but a contract of responsibility exists from the moment of birth, which is in part enforceable by law and is a powerful social custom. Among friends, employers, and employees, however, our connections include a mix of stated and implied agreements worked out in advance or over time. Greater and lesser degrees of intimacy depend on factors such as how much trust and contact exists. We also have many brief or superficial contacts with others—store clerks, public figures, neighbors—where not much bonding is felt. What we get from them or give them is more or less a matter of routine—a smile and money in exchange for goods, applause for a song.

We all vary in our relationships. One person may be deeply bonded with people or pets, while another may be surrounded by generations of relatives. Some may feel a strong sense of obligation and commitment toward family members, even if all feelings of bonding are strained or broken. Some acknowledge only a very few strong connections—one or two relationships—and prefer to have only superficial contact with everybody else. What satisfies and fulfills one person may seem bleak fare to someone else.

How, then, do we determine what is reasonable to expect, of ourselves and others? What do we say to those who vocally insist we owe them, whether we like it or not? Where do we draw the line?

One of the goals in Step 8 is to develop a sane present perspective on the relationships we have, and have had with others. What's needed is a spiritual standpoint that makes it clear, at least to us, where we stand in relation to others. If we don't have this, we can only guess at our responsibility—or remain a pawn to the demands of others.

In Step 8, as in all of the Steps, we focus on our own experience, and we review the boundaries of intimacy and commitment we learned and rehearsed growing up. However fuzzily they may have been stated or understood, we did learn some boundaries and limits on what to expect from others in our family system. What were they? And did we get what we needed to be whole and healthy spiritual beings by using that set of rules? Were our spiritual rights to feel loved, nurtured, included and recognized, respected and celebrated—or were they violated, neglected, denied?

We come to see the spiritual underpinnings of each one of our relationships more clearly, past and present, if we imagine ourselves at the very center of a circle that includes all of our relationships. Everyone in our circle is a valuable, unique spiritual being. No matter how distorted our relationship may have become due to the effects of addictions, compulsions, or codependencies, this is still true.

If we are willing to think of ourselves as having entered life at the center of such a circle, grounded in universal good will, we will be able to evaluate our relationships, thinking in terms of what we had a reasonable right to expect, and of what we did, or didn't get. All those within our circle, we think, have some degree of responsibility to us, and we to them, even if it's only to acknowledge our mutual right to be alive.

Our job in Step 8 is to determine the boundaries separating the different kinds of relationships we have and have had, to admit where we've been let down or where we have failed others, and then to become willing to act in the present based upon this new perspective. We aren't dependent upon others in doing this. From the center of our own circle, we are free to investigate and to act—whether others do or not—to heal our circle of relationships.

Let's look at the kinds of relationships we have as human beings. First, there were those who were our primary caregivers—our parents or those who took that role. We had the deepest need and right to expect unconditional love, nurturing, guidance, and companionship from these individuals from the very beginning of our life. Later, as parents, we become the primary caregivers to our own children and in some respects to our partners. From these relationships we gain or fail to gain the strongest validation of our authentic selves. This is our primary circle.

Beyond the boundary of these primary contacts, but still very intimately involved in our lives, are trusted intimates—siblings, grandparents, or others who are deeply committed to us. Trusted intimates have a great influence in our lives, too. They are expected to give us practical help as well as dependable loyalty. Although they are committed to us, they aren't our primary caregivers. They have other responsibilities and interests that we must recognize and accept. If these limits become blurred, issues of authority and abandonment result. As adults, our trusted intimates probably include our closest friends and family members who are committed to stick with us.

Outside the boundaries of this circle there are those who have some influence on us—aunts, uncles, cousins, family friends and, later, the friends we make for ourselves. These are secondary, extended family relationships. Limits of commitment in these relationships vary, depending on a range of factors including which ethnic group we identify with. Generally, these people aren't responsible for meeting our material needs, except for perhaps an occasional helping hand. Mutual loyalty and companionship are the important responsibilities in this circle. So are shared activities and voluntary cooperative efforts. As adults, relationships we form at work, church, or other places where interests are shared may become, in effect, part of our extended family ties. We practice recognizing, negotiating, and respecting each other's limits and boundaries in this circle. If we lack an extended family growing up, then we may tend to isolate ourselves from groups as adults. We may also confuse the companionship of shared activities with deeper commitments. This can lead to social confusion. Overcommitment, inappropriate disclosures, and/or a tendency to impose, overreact to, or flee from social stresses can result.

Finally, there is a fourth circle, made up of non-intimate elders and authorities in our community. These are our role models. They inspire our confidence and respect. Teachers, doctors, ministers, and heroes such as athletes and public figures are within this circle. Although little day-to-day companionship may be involved in these relationships, we still learn from them. We give respect and learn to earn respect through relating to these leaders and the ideals they represent. If our family system boundaries cut us off from or restrict our identification with this fourth circle, we may feel we are part of an underclass group.

Now we reflect on our own situation—our family and other relationships. Did we have all four kinds of relationships growing up, or were there some holes? What about today? We're interested in seeing just what we learned, or missed, about receiving and giving care, support, and recognition in our childhood environment. It may be helpful to create a chart. Substitute the actual relationships you did have, in each layer, with real names, rather than categories.

Questions to Ponder

1. Who let you down? Who hurt you? Who taught you to be a victim?

2. Whom have you carried these behaviors over to in your life? Whom have you let down, abandoned, or abused?

3. Is there someone you can't forgive?

4. Is there someone you can't forget?

STEP NINE

We make direct amends to such people wherever possible, except when to do so would injure them or others.

A newcomer asked me, "When am I going to get happy in this program?" I said, "Nothing to it. Just stop doing whatever it is that's making you unhappy. That'll do the trick."

—Clay S., A.A. "Old timer"

In recovery I no longer run to Mom—knowing she'll invalidate me. I also resist calling everyone who may be sympathetic, when my real motive is simply to stimulate my own outrage. As I remain unwilling to contribute to my family's dysfunctional dynamic, it ceases to affect me one day at a time.

—Charlie T., Humboldt, CA

Making amends—to ourselves and to others—in recovery always means taking appropriate action. Appropriate action, as defined in Step 9, is never manipulation or revenge, nor does it involve the loss of self-respect. Whether the end result is acknowledging a debt to be repaid or requires substituting honest communication for hurtful defensiveness or appeasement in a relationship makes no difference. Step 9 challenges us to act in ways that take courage. It also asks us to let our Higher Power guide us when it comes to timing our amends. If we are willing to meet the challenge of Step 9, our very willingness takes us to fuller selfhood of sanity.

In Step 9, appropriate actions are always actions that build self-esteem. Even when they may involve making a difficult choice or may not produce an immediate healing in our relationships, making amends still produces feelings which are deeply satisfying and empowering. When we act appropriately in Step 9, our actions are the acts of our recovered inner self. They are initiated in our hearts and carried out with the deliberate courage of a clear mind guided by a loving God. This is very different from merely making apologies or reacting to pressures.

There are three factors we must balance in each amends we will make.

1. All of our amends should reflect our own innermost values that we've identified.

2. When we make amends, we must stay within the healthy limits we have established for ourselves.

3. When we reach out to others, we need to remember to honor and respect their boundaries and values.

Even though each of these goals is simple, putting them into practice can take some planning. If we have a plan, we'll feel more assured when we approach people. We will see Step 9 as a process with a beginning and an end. Not only will we be less inclined to approach Step 9 in a secretive or haphazard way, we'll be much less likely to skip over some people on our list or to drag the process on indefinitely.

Step 9 is the final act of the work we began with the Inventory process. If we have worked the Steps leading up to this one, we will have a pretty clear idea of who we are and where we want to go with our lives. In Step 8, we made a list of those who were harmed by our old way of living.

Now in Step 9 we consider what is appropriate to share with each of them, in terms of offering amends.

It's a good idea to go over our entire list with a sponsor or trusted ally as we begin this Step. Usually, it simplifies matters if we separate the list into several classes of people: those who are still a part of our lives; those who have moved on (or died); employers or other more or less impersonal authorities; those we still don't like.

There may be some on our list whom we have already approached—those with whom we have close ties or those whom we have felt a keen sense of remorse toward. In working a formal amends Step, we review what we have said and done already in these cases. Have our amends up to this point been in any way haphazard, self-attacking, appeasing, or manipulative? Have we honored the boundaries of others in making these amends? Have we been insensitive? Having worked all of the Steps that lead up to amends now, do we see anything that needs to be changed, reconsidered, or revised? We do ourselves and our loved ones a kindness if we reconsider positive new ways that recovery can impact these relationships.

Now, going on to others on our list, we consider how we can straighten out our end of the trouble. Are feelings still raw? Is a letter more appropriate than a visit? Is the timing right?

If we are considering amends where undiscovered secrets or criminal activities have been involved, it's desirable to discuss the whole matter with a sponsor before taking any direct action. What sort of crime or secret is involved? What role did addiction or codependent patterns have in the incident? Were others involved or would others be implicated if the whole matter came out? What is the path of greatest healing? It is wise to wait until clarity prevails before taking any drastic action in such cases. We need to listen for spiritual guidance so that healing, not added injury, comes from the amends we make.

In cases where we have slandered or abused the trust of others, especially those we still dislike, delay is practically never justified. Tempted as we may be to write off these wrongs, taking an easy way out really defeats the purpose of Step 9. We only retreat into old habits of isolation when we try to justify ignoring some of the people that we've hurt.

Our purpose in making amends is not to take the inventories of those we've hurt. We don't have to expose ourselves to further injury if they are unreceptive to spiritually centered communication. We are offering amends to acknowledge the ways that we have acted out or reacted codependently to them. When we do this, we are unhooking ourselves from those old errors that we now see clearly. If we are to move on, free of the accumulated burden of past errors, nothing short of direct action guided by a loving God will do. We have to live our recoveries so that our ideals become the substance of experience in our lives. Step 9 is the way we unify what we believe with who we are. "Faith without works is dead."

We may be very willing to go ahead with the amends process but, as long-time victims, we may still be inclined to guess at what it means to be "normal" in some, or many, areas of living. We may feel that we lack the necessary footing to make balanced judgments. We may also lack confidence and be inclined to give in to the demands or opinions of others. How are we to decide between our own wishes and the pulls and tugs of others who may want more than we are prepared to give? We may wish that we could find some sort of formula for keeping our balance when it comes to interacting with others.

Notice that the exercise of good judgment produces actions which affirm strong, spiritually centered identities. Using good judgment means acting from a basis which is in touch with the principles we have today, but which leaves us room to learn something, too. When we become established in a genuinely functional way of dealing with life, we feel secure and not so threatened by others. The self-respect that doesn't depend on being "one-up" is rooted in this security. We feel independent, not isolated. We can care for people and appreciate them for who they are.

On the other hand, being judgmental is a fear-based reaction where we try to enforce our idea of what's right on others. Most often, we become judgmental when we feel threatened. Situations that put us in touch with losses of the past often feel confusing for this reason. When we are making amends with people who share painful history with us, it helps to stick with some definite communication goals, at least at first. If communication during an amends starts to feel threatening, affirming something positive can help. Sticking with "I" statements is also a good bet. Fear of other people tends to lessen as we get more comfortable communicating from our end. And as our lives and relationships begin to heal, making amends becomes a way out of trouble that feels good instead of a source of anxiety.

Finally, what do we owe ourselves, in terms of direct amends? For one thing, we probably had pretty limited ideas about what is desirable, or possible, for ourselves. It's likely that we've taken in some nasty, judgmental attitudes toward ourselves. Perhaps we've acted out the negative messages we got from others. For instance, while addicts are poisoning themselves with drugs or alcohol they are usually telling themselves that they are no damn good. Codependents tell themselves that they're to blame or that everything would be fine if only they were perfect. These ideas are poison, too.

Certainly we owe ourselves amends for all these put-down messages. Most of us will say that when we stop the abuse we are making amends to ourselves. Surely, this is true. But don't we deserve something more than an end to taking some form of poison? Aren't there some positive acts we can take to make up for having undercut ourselves?

If we missed out on something in life that we wanted, do we love ourselves enough to reach out for it now? Perhaps we want to go to college or we want to relate in a way that we've been afraid to risk before. Can we do it now? Or if it's something that can't be reclaimed, is there something else we want? If we are going to forgive ourselves for whatever we've lost or missed out on, we must actively seek to bring renewed joy and contentment to the lives we now create. If we ask our Higher Power's help, we will surely be guided on such a path. A most important amends we owe ourselves is our willingness to let go of limited ideas of what is possible.

Some of us will come to see that we were, indeed, very badly treated by others who, at one time, had power over us. What can be done about these old harms? Injuries from abuse, neglect, or lack of commitment from parents or mates may seem impossible to forgive. Maybe we've been victims of prejudice or discrimination. We don't try to justify the injuries others have done us in Step 9. That would be as unjust as trying to rationalize the abuses we have passed along ourselves. We don't go back into denial about the problems that really did exist and may still. But we need not leave these old tyrants in control of our destinies. Even if they remain sick or abusive, we can make amends to ourselves by beginning to draw our validation directly from God.

We perform a generous act of amends to ourselves and to those who have done us harm when we go ahead and heal. It's a kind act not to let ourselves be destroyed by the diseased actions of others. It's even kinder when we are able to fully embrace success as something we can accept in our lives. This is true, too, for the effects of social prejudices and abuses. When a healthy life becomes "normal" then we have healed, no matter how bad things may have been once. As we free ourselves, we also lighten the burden of those who let us down. This is a very kind thing to do.

We have only to claim success, joy, health, and abundance and turn to our Higher Power for it. As we do this—and it may take a little persistence to get used to the idea—we find that no one stands in our way. We may feel a measure of grief as we begin to give ourselves this new outlook on life. We may wish we had taken action sooner and not missed out on opportunities or wasted years of our lives. To some extent, feeling remorse is unavoidable if we've been making mistakes in our way of living. But we can do a lot to make amends for time we feel has been wasted by sharing our stories with others. Maybe some-one else won't find it necessary to re-invent the wheel in the same way we have! In this way, even our failures become resources in the lives around us as we share our-selves in the fellowship of the spirit.

Questions to Ponder

1. What appropriate actions can I take now to heal or repair the past?

2. Is this action free of appeasement or manipulation?

3. Is this action free of self-righteousness?

4. Is the timing right?

STEP TEN

We continue to take personal inventory, and when we are wrong, we promptly admit it.

The idea that we can be possessively loving of a few, can ignore the many, and can continue to fear or hate anybody, has to be abandoned, if only a little at a time.

—12 Steps and 12 Traditions

When it seems like the same things are happening again, it's important that I remember I'm not the same, vulnerable, three-foot-tall little person I was then.

—Brenda, Maui, HI

Step 10 is the first of three maintenance Steps in recovery—along with Steps 11 and 12. These three Steps encourage interlocking practices which help to safeguard our recoveries from complacency and forgetfulness. These Steps help us to stay spiritually fit, a day at a time.

The first one, Step 10, asks us to stay self-aware in the present. It also asks us to be willing to act in the present, based on our awareness. Step 10 serves to remind us that recovery is a way of life, not an event that happens and is left behind.

No matter what we learn, it seems true that we keep only what we practice. This is as true of the self-awareness skills we learn in recovery as it is of a tennis backstroke. In recovery from addictions, compulsions, or codependency, we have to continue to build habits of self-scrutiny to be applied on an as-we-go basis. If we don't, old behaviors and attitudes—ruts worn by years of practice—soon begin to creep back into our lives. Our vision of personal freedom may quickly become blurred. Despite all insight and intentions to the contrary, we may find ourselves making the same mistakes all over again, reacting as we did before recovery.

As people in recovery, we have to learn to live life on life's terms. Life wouldn't be life if it did not include challenges, surprises, reminders of the past, even some sadness and tragedy. Daily events and the pace of life can chip into serenity, leaving us agitated, fearful, frustrated. Before our recovery, we may have had a front of dishonest behaviors we used to create a false appearance under stress, stuffing our honest feelings and disguising our motives. Now that we are no longer content to stuff our feelings or to lie to ourselves about our motives, we may feel unsure how to act. Do we act from feelings or not?

Of course, basing actions on purely automatic, impulsive reactions to daily events and stresses can get us into trouble. We come to realize more and more that feeling our feelings and acting them out on others are two entirely different things. Impulse may prompt us to react from fear, projection, jealousy, spite. Honest as these feelings may be, acting on them is likely to cause pain and confusion. Most of us, too, have personal sensitivities that make us more prone to react unpredictably. We may be inclined to justify becoming touchy and defensive in some areas.

If we are resolved to take off our stuffed-feelings masks and become more honest communicators in recovery, a process of trial and error may be expected. And any time we change and grow, we can expect to make mistakes.

In order to minimize the accumulation and impact of the wreckage of the present we create in our lives, we need to find ways to keep an eye on our own conduct. Working Step 10 helps us to take responsibility for both our successes and our failed attempts in the present. We learn to "take our own inventory" on an ongoing basis. We own our progress, as we admit and correct our failings and missteps. In doing this, we accept responsibility for monitoring our own conduct. As we become increasingly aware of our own vulnerability pitfalls, we find ways to walk around them in the present. Self-inventory provides a "self-rescuing kit" to get us back on the path that leads in the direction we choose.

Self-inventory involves engaging in a kind of constructive self-criticism. Many of us feel fearful and defensive under any form of real or implied criticism, however, even if it's coming from ourselves. We may still have painful memories of criticisms being used against us, as justification for abuse or abandonment. We may not have a clear sense of the role constructive criticism plays in skill-building or in achieving goals.

Constructive criticism is a key factor in the learning process. When we establish a goal for ourselves—whether that goal is personal recovery or something more specific, say, learning to drive a car—then a strategy needs to be set up for achieving that goal. A goal without strategy and objectives for achieving it remains only a fantasy.

In the goal of learning to drive, talking about wanting to learn to drive is not a strategy for learning to drive. An effective strategy involves something definite, such as signing up to take a driver's education course. Driver's education is a strategy for learning to drive. If it's a good course, it will be laid out in a series of smaller objectives that are designed to help us move, little by little, toward our goal. If we want to succeed and become licensed drivers, we have to be teachable and make use of the feedback we get as we go along. Utilizing feedback, including feedback in the form of constructive criticism, is an important part of getting where we want to go.

In the 12-Step programs, our goal is sane and balanced living, and the program is a strategy designed to help us achieve this aim. The Steps are markers along the path, even though we each move independently and make our own choices. To stay on the path, we have to pay attention to how we progress. We still need to be teachable. We need to give ourselves permission to claim our progress and validate our feelings. At the same time, we need to remain as objective as we can about how our behaviors match up with our recovery goals.

Developing the habit of constructive self-reflection does, admittedly, take practice. But once we accept the idea that this act of self-discipline is not intended as torturing self-attack, then we can begin to view Step 10 as an act of self-protection and personal care. Choosing to keep up a discipline we have taken on voluntarily builds self-respect and deepens self-trust. We come to experience ourselves as persons capable of commitment, which is a big factor for building confidence and personal security. Instead of a dreaded and dreary bout of self-attack, the reparenting we give ourselves in Step 10 gives us clarity about our own motives and keeps us focused on our goals. Getting realistic about ourselves usually makes us less sensitive to the critical feedback we receive from others, too.

Resistance to Step 10 often shows up as resistance to doing the inventory now. We may be inclined to put it off. Won't we, some ask, squelch all spontaneity if we have to watch our every move, worry about our every word? But taking a spot-check is not intended to stifle creativity. Overcoming this sort of resistance to Step 10 is largely a matter of taking the actions we believe will serve us in recovery and trusting that our feelings will catch up later. When we get in the habit of regularly doing Step 10, usually more creativity becomes possible, not less. Structure is healthy self-responsibility, an antidote to codependent control.

When we take an inventory depends upon circumstances. Taking a spot-check of our feelings and motives is an option, not an obligation. When stress or hostility begins to dominate a situation, we can immediately choose to take a few deep breaths before we speak, while we examine what we are feeling. We bring the focus back to ourselves: What is our goal in this situation? Do our present feelings prompt us to want to act in ways that aren't in line with our goals or commitments in the situation? Are we communicating honestly—asking for what we really want, offering what we actually want to give? What are some options? Can we, for example, act to refocus the interaction in a more positive way? Does wisdom dictate that we temporarily remove ourselves until emotions settle? Taking a few seconds to spot-check is an exercise of our freedom to choose.

There are periodic inventories that can be very helpful, too. At day's end, we may take a few minutes to reflect, with a notepad, on how our day has gone. If we are inclined to do so, even 15 minutes of journaling or sketching can be a very helpful form of inventory. Buried feelings may often surface when we give our Inner Child a few minutes for free expression.

It's a good practice to ask ourselves a few questions aimed at the areas where there may have been difficulties or triumphs:

1. Have I isolated myself today? Have I taken a communication risk?
2. Have I been obsessed with something—a person, food, drugs, power? Have I been relieved of an obsession?
3. Have I felt like a victim today, weaker than or controlled by others? Have I held my own?
4. Have I appeased or injured someone today? Have I acted from my inner loyalties today and kept my boundaries intact?
5. Have I been dishonest—stuffed or denied any feelings today? Have I been willing to feel all of my feelings?
6. Was I distracted today—did I lose touch with my Higher Power due to stress, anger, or fear? Did I trust my Higher Power under difficult circumstances?

We are careful to own our progress in these areas of daily living. It's as important to give ourselves credit for the gains we make as it is for us to admit where we have fallen short. In owning our progress we are giving credit to the power of healing in our lives.

It is also helpful to do a periodic review of our progress over a longer time frame—a month, several months, a year. Many find that a few days of retreat, taking some special, personal time for deeper reflection, is a form of self-care that is very nurturing. It is often the case that our here-and-now issues have roots that can be traced back to past incidents. It's a good practice to return to Step 4 periodically when previously undiscovered aspects of the past begin to surface. Often, we are given new insight as recovery progresses and we become spiritually grounded to deal with deeper levels of truth about ourselves and our histories.

Step 10 is a here-and-now action Step. If we are to gain the benefits of this work, we have to remain willing to act in the present. If we avoid or postpone taking action now to correct the errors we uncover in Step 10, we are getting in our own way. We get to keep only what we practice. If we don't make progress in building a new, positive way of life, as compulsive personalities, we tend to revert rapidly to our old, latent behaviors.

We needn't fear that we will fail to meet a false, perfectionistic standard in Step 10. It is not an outside authority that we answer to when we act with honesty to clear up our end of a problem. Our Inner Child's awakened conscience prompts us to act.

Sometimes, the ways we have been wrong may be in the acts we haven't taken. We may have been afraid to risk asking a question or exposing a caring feeling to someone because we feared rejection or thought we might look foolish. Perhaps we haven't given someone something of ourselves out of self-protective fear. Our strengthened Inner

Child may prompt us to take action to extend ourselves in ways that are new and wonderful—and also risky. We have to remember to be patient with ourselves in this phase of our recovery. Our Inner Child deserves to be parented with gentleness. It's important that we take only the risks to feel and share that we are prepared to leave in the care of our Higher Power. If we find that we are afraid to trust the outcome to the God of our understanding, then we may not be ready to take the risk.

We are careful not to sabotage ourselves by needlessly setting ourselves up for invalidation or abuse. But we remind ourselves that recovery isn't a fantasy or a fairytale, either. Some of our risks and disclosures may be rejected or misunderstood, or we may not be able to communicate as we hoped we could. In living life on life's terms, honest action combined with trust in a loving God will see us through. A sense of humor is a form of faith that can be cultivated, too. Our aim is to heed the guidance of our Higher Power as we feel it in our heart, and take the action our awakened conscience dictates. If we take action to make working Step 10 a part of our lives today, we can safely leave the outcome of our efforts in the care of a loving God.

Questions to Ponder

1. Review today (so far) and notice how you have felt, or if you've been stuffing any feelings. Feel those now.

2. Which issues are involved? (Be as specific as you can.) If you are in the midst of your day, make yourself an affirmation for the area (or areas) that are giving you trouble and repeat this to yourself several times, perhaps alternating with the Serenity Prayer or other favorite.

3. When you have time, explore the issue or issues involved. Do memories or feelings from the past come up for you?

4. Are you powerless in some respects involving this issue? Is this an issue that takes you back to Step 1, or 4, or 6?

STEP ELEVEN

We seek through prayer and meditation to improve our conscious contact with God as we understand God, praying only for knowledge of God's will for us and power to carry that out.

Nan-in, a Japanese Zen master, poured tea for his visitor. He filled the cup, and then kept on pouring. The visitor watched until he could contain himself no more. "Look! It's overfull. No more can go in!" "Like this cup," Nan-in responded, "you, too, are full of your own speculations. How can I show you Zen unless you first empty your cup?"

—Muju

Well, you see: once upon a time there was a blazing fire inside me. The cold could do nothing against it, a youthfulness, a spring no autumn could touch.... There was an enormous energy there....A force, it must have been the life force, mustn't it?...And then it grew weaker and it all died away ..

—Eugene Ionesco

Personal recovery in any 12-Step program can be described as a spiritual journey from a kind of spiritual death back into life. We who were the lost people—victims of addictions or codependent patterns—rediscover our authentic, inner selves again. We move from the bleak, barren landscapes of a failed existence back into a fruitful way of life, full of challenge and opportunity.

Connecting with our lost inner identity, the magical Inner Child within, is a spiritual process. However much therapy, medical treatment, hard work, and good sponsorship may provide, the actual experience of healing requires connecting with a deeply spiritual core within ourselves. What makes recovery a reality is the fire of vitality that is reawakened in us. As much as we may gratefully acknowledge the skilled guidance and support we receive from others, it still remains that all of this would count for little if no spark of fire within ourselves existed to respond.

To build a strong connection to the resources we have within, the flame of spirit within us needs to be fueled if it is to burn with a steady light. Working Step 11 is a way to feed the contact between our ordinary awareness and our spiritual power source within. Making regular use of prayer and meditation is a maintenance practice that helps keep us in touch with personal inspiration.

Even if we are willing to acknowledge the importance of spirituality in recovery, we may still have a certain amount of resistance to the idea of prayer—or to the systematic practice of it. In order to begin to integrate the practice of prayer into our daily lives as Step 11 recommends, we may need to reconsider the meaning and purpose of prayer. What has prayer meant to us in the past?

Painful associations can easily block the way to utilizing prayer or wanting to take time for it. Perhaps we associate humiliating memories with prayer—memories of begging God or of trying in vain to strike a deal with God to stave off a disaster. Why weren't our prayers answered? Weren't we good enough? Or did we fail, somehow? We may feel unwilling to try prayer again—as though we are facing the possibility of a kind of soul-rejection if we do.

Maybe we were exposed to prayer in a household where appearances were everything and emotions were suppressed. We may have memories of prayer as a ritual smothering the Child within. We may have come to look on prayer as an undertaking intended mainly to impress others or to keep from being criticized. We may remember prayer as a mechanical repeating of mere words, hollow rituals devoid of meaning, feelings, or power. If we experienced much religious hypocrisy in the past, we may fear that turning to prayer represents a kind of self-negation.

If we are tormented by these or similar associations with the idea of prayer, our first response to Step 11 is likely to be a form of inner resistance—avoidance, defiance, or denial. We remind ourselves that resistance is often an indicator of a need to unbrick more inner walls and feel the feelings that have been stuffed away. We may need to begin working Step 11 by giving ourselves permission to grieve the pain of confusion and loss that is locked inside ourselves and that is associated with old ideas about prayer.

We can help ourselves by redefining our understanding of prayer now. We can take the initiative to reparent our Inner Child with a more realistic understanding, one that is no longer hooked to vain pleading or self-abasement. The *New Century Dictionary* (1957, Appleton-Century-Crofts, Inc.) tells us that prayer is "communication directed toward God [including]...asking, praising, adoring, confessing." Regardless of any confusion which we may have associated with the idea, prayer really isn't so complicated, after all. Prayer is the act of extending ourselves toward the God of our understanding. It's a matter of how we conceive of God and of our relationship to the spiritual that determines if and how we pray and what form those prayers will take.

If we work to replace any old conceptions we might have of a weak or mean God with a kinder understanding, then reaching out to our Higher Power becomes easier. A Higher (or Inner) Power that is both capable and willing to support us is an ally that we want to reach. When we pray, we affirm our personal right to communicate with the God of our understanding. Few rights rival this one, in terms of power in our lives.

How and when we pray is up to us. We may or may not feel it is appropriate to get down upon our knees in prayer. Rituals such as ceremony, dance, assuming particular postures, or going to special places—shrines, churches, grottos—are all left to individual conscience in 12-Step programs. Praying in a group, including saying the Serenity Prayer at the beginning of 12-Step meetings, is never an obligation. These personal decisions are always a matter of free choice. In all 12-Step programs we are assured of our right to a personal relationship with the God of our understanding. As we develop that relationship, we pray in words, dance, ritual ceremony, song, or whatever comes from our hearts. If we don't have a positive association with forms of prayer we learned in childhood, Step 11 is an opportunity to explore new options.

We may find ways to claim as prayer some activities that we may not have associated with concepts of prayer before. Affirmations, for instance, are a positive form of prayer that asks by affirming that God is willing and able to see us made whole. Affirmations, many find, are a spiritual antidote to many old ideas about God and about prayer. Repeating (or writing) affirmations directly contradicts old behavior hangovers we may carry. We no longer beg an external force when we pray in affirmations. Instead, we join ourselves with the God/Spirit that dwells within us.

Rejoicing in our blessings is another form of prayer we may not have claimed. When we express (inwardly or outwardly) our gratitude for the good things we see around us—the pleasures of restored health and sanity, the joy we feel in fellowship—we are doing what the dictionary defines as praising and rejoicing. When we appreciate a sunset or feel awe in the face of nature, talent, or courage and we acknowledge the spiritual basis of these wonders, we are also praising God.

If we begin to claim these forms of prayer and worship, we may find that we have always been pretty spiritual folks. Many of us find when we review memories of childhood, that we praised the beauty of life, even if we had no words to express the reverent feelings within our hearts. What little child has not, in his/her peaceful moments, delighted in life? We can choose to count among our prayers our appreciation for a waterfall, or for a bird's song, the sounds of children's laughter, the smell of dinner cooking. We can choose to see the work we do as a prayer of offering we make with our bodies and our minds, a praise to our Higher Power that gives us energy and direction. The love we give to others can be a prayer if we see it as a validation of spirit that flows from heart to heart.

Once we have come to understand prayer as a right we enjoy, rather than as a burden or an obligation, then the whole activity begins to take on a natural harmony in our lives. We find building and improving a conscious contact with the God of our understanding is no longer an activity that takes us away from life. Instead, prayer becomes an integrated pulsebeat that gradually comes to underlay much of what we do.

Step 11 also asks us to practice meditation to improve our conscious contact with the God of our understanding. If prayer is the act of reaching out to God, then meditation can be seen as the act of letting Spirit in. When we take time to meditate, we make a conscious decision to open ourselves to guidance and inspiration.

One of the classic methods of meditating is the practice of clearing the mind of all thought. All distractions, including emotional responses to thoughts, are gradually released, dismissed. The object of classical meditation is emptiness, stillness, complete one-pointedness of being. Achieving this state of poised detachment may be the goal of years of discipline.

But meditation need not be so formal nor so thoroughgoing to be effective. Our goal, in Step 11, is just to make some space and time available in our schedules to receive new direction. Meditation involves making a decision to set aside our projects, goals, and other commitments for a few minutes and to use that time receptively. Rather than attempting to become entirely devoid of all thought, most find it easier to simply replace the usual preoccupations of the mind with something else. Inspirational reading or repeating a brief, affirmative statement (mantra) can refocus our awareness and create a quiet space within. Making a decision to suspend action and worry while listening to a piece of music or a meditation tape is another good approach. Yoga, rhythmic programs of exercise, jogging, drawing, making pottery, lying in the cool grass contemplating the clouds that sail across the sky—any of these practices can be used in meditation, so long as we make a conscious decision to release our everyday cares and ambitions while we do them.

Once we see that meditation need not be the rigorous practice of a demanding discipline, the practice usually feels less intimidating. We may nonetheless, still be inclined to postpone or forget to give ourselves quiet breaks.

Keeping ourselves distracted—out of our bodies to a greater or lesser extent—can be a defense. We may have learned to stuff pain, fear, or grief by focusing on something else, on something outside of ourselves or on a different feeling. When we lived lives that were dominated by addiction, our Inner Child within simply had to escape from the pain of a present that s/he was powerless to change. Without necessarily making a conscious decision, we found ways to escape. We coped and survived.

Coping by escaping from the now is a habit that, once established, often dies hard. Individuals in recovery may admit that they have been more or less addicted to excitement—to anger, to silent rehearsals of dialogue with people who aren't present, to fantasies of fear, worry, domination, or conquest. These distractions cut us off from experiencing the responses of our authentic selves within. To compound the confusion, we may also have become magnets generating or gravitating toward real crisis in our lives and relationships. We may act out our fantasies, live out our fears.

Meditation is a practice that directly contradicts all these forms of distraction. When we meditate, we give ourselves permission to be 100 percent in the present, here and now. We give ourselves over to the care of God as we understand God. We consciously release our hold upon everything. For those of us who have carried self-protective excitement habits along into recovery, meditation may threaten something near and dear to us—our ability to escape from feelings in the present.

Rather than blaming ourselves as failures who are unable to work Step 11, we need to see our old coping mechanisms for what they were—the way we survived an impossible past. Under past circumstances, escape was probably in order. We lacked other tools. Now, if we are willing to use them, we have tools available to us. We don't have to run.

A good beginning is simply to take a few minutes to breathe deeply while we go over the ways it is now safe to be in the present. How has our life changed? How are we different? We may still feel like rebelling, but gentle, persistent reparenting will usually succeed better than insistent demands. As we note the ways that we are now safe to be our undefended selves, we reassure our Child within that the experience of recovery is lasting and trustworthy. This may take a little time, but, fortunately for us, the Child within wants to be present in the now. The Child within has gifts for us: creativity, innocence, a sense of fun.

Re-entering the present as an undefended, vulnerable human being is risky but essential. Playful forms of meditation are good ways to rebond with our inner self. As we gradually replace distraction with meditation, our Inner Child returns.

Seeking to discover and live out "God's will for us..." is basic to recovery. We who lost touch with our authentic inner self find that this connection is restored as addictions, compulsions, and codependent patterns fall away. What is most authentic about each of us is primarily spiritual in nature. In the continued practice of Step 11, we seek gradually to reduce the inner conflict that interferes with contact with our authentic self. When momentary goals take us away from this larger goal, we remind ourselves of the purpose of Step 11. Lasting success depends upon sticking with our truest selves. We need to remember not to abandon ourselves. When in doubt, we ask, "Is this goal (or impulse) in keeping with my highest good?" We seek direct validation by means of prayer, along with the power to live by what we discover is written in our hearts. In Step 11, we seek guidance so that our actions cease to be rooted in reaction to forces outside of ourselves. We move in the direction of balance and poise, toward being in touch with a comfortable sense of purpose and inner harmony.

As we become more and more willing to practice Step 11 and to live from the guidance we receive, we tend naturally to experience a growing feeling of confidence. We usually notice increased tolerance toward others. Finding inner validation, we no longer feel so fearful of making or acknowledging mistakes. We no longer have to guess at what to do or say, nor do we second-guess others to gain their approval or divert their wrath. Even sadness and pain eventually lose some of their force in our lives. Fear of these feelings or shame about having them begins to evaporate in the strong light of Spirit.

As we come to live more on spiritual power, directing our will toward conscious contact with the God of our understanding, we find more of the courage necessary to face our lives with honesty—and humor. After all, spiritual power is an inexhaustible wellspring that has been made available to us, a day at a time. We come to understand that we needn't fear—or hate. With prayer and meditation to keep our contact with our Source, we may truly come to walk in peace. And as we accept ourselves as worthy of this peace, we may discover previously unrecognized talents and gifts within ourselves.

Questions to Ponder

1. Is prayer a word with meaning for you?
2. Do you feel you can meditate?
3. What does conscious contact feel like? How does it show up in your life?
4. Is knowledge of God's will something you sense inside yourself? How about power?

STEP TWELVE

Having had a spiritual awakening as a result of these Steps, we try to carry this message to others and to practice these principles in all of our affairs.

People of genius are rarely content browsing upon the greatness of their own thoughts...More than most, such people are called by the mighty herd instinct; their searchings, their findings, and their calls are inexorably meant for the crowd and must be heard.

—Dr. Carl Gustav Jung

Perhaps one day I may even make a commitment to serve a group, and even (gulp) get involved and active...I'm beginning to understand that the Area Meeting Schedule, the office, and the phone system don't happen by magic.

—Anonymous, Portland ACoA

Human beings depend upon each other. We are born tiny and helpless. Our families and community must sustain us during a long period if we are to survive at all. As adults, as parents and productive members of our societies, we assume the roles of providers. Living long, we at last come to depend again upon the care of others as vitality gradually fades. Our lives move to a nearly audible pulse of changing needs, changing goals, through a life dance that is linked and entwined with the lives of others.

Coming to recognize ourselves as a part of life's inter-dependent dance is a mark of maturity. If we accept ourselves as valuable, we come to see ourselves as worthy of the love and care necessary for our well-being. We cease to feel shamed by our needs. We accept what we need to be whole from life and from others, and we also come to accept ourselves as having the capacity to give. We come to see that we share a responsibility to put something back, if what we have received is to be there for the next person or for the next generation.

Much of the maintenance work that we do in Step 12 is about putting something back. It is not based in a joyless sense of obligation, though. We offer to share the way of life we have found in the give and take of life's dance. What we give, we give voluntarily, offering to reach out our hand to the next person who reaches out for help.

Our service and 12-Step work is based on the realization that spiritual insights quickly lose force unless these insights become the basis of action in our lives. We do the work of Step 12 in order to keep what we have, by living what we have learned. As we share what we have gained through recovery, we reaffirm the changes that have taken place in our lives.

"Spiritual awakening" in 12-Step programs starts with learning something about humility. In 12-Step programs, we come together in a healing process that begins with admitting what we can't do for ourselves. The price of admission to our fellowship is a depth of honesty that is painful to accept. We each must face a question we'd rather not answer: Has physical, mental, or emotional addiction rendered us helpless—powerless to stop doing what is harming us, while we are at the same time unable to go on as we were?

The willingness to even consider the question of Step 1 requires reflecting on profound spiritual issues. Addictions, after all, are defined as life-threatening conditions. If we admit we are powerless over some form of addiction, aren't we facing the possibility of our own death or a kind of living death? Stripped of denial, we feel naked. We are powerless, out of control—as vulnerable as newborns in a new world.

A spiritual awakening begins when, despite our reluctance and fear, we actually take Step 1. Starting with our first honest admission that we really do have a problem, we begin to move out of self-loss. Admitting an unattractive truth that is threatening to our inner sense of security and our image takes courage. We can't know in advance if we will recover. We face the terrors of uncertainty. Risking action in the face of uncertainty, when life itself may be at stake, requires acting in faith. This combination of honesty, courage, and the willingness to act in faith is the basis of a spiritual way of life.

Spiritual awakening develops as we reconnect with our authentic inner self, the Inner Child. All of the Steps include some of what we mean in Step 12. From the first time we share at a meeting, we are beginning to carry the message. We share our experience, including our pain, our unflattering insights into our own motivations, the feelings we fear others will not accept. Others who haven't found the courage to face similar features in themselves may be helped by identifying with what we've shared.

When we speak from our hearts, those who share a common problem hear us and are comforted. Whether it's a common experience or shared feelings that run through dissimilar events doesn't seem to matter. Without attempting to impress anyone, we always have something to give when we share our truth. And in the act of personal sharing, we awaken more and more to our spiritual identity, validating and claiming ourselves.

Having this spiritual awakening is an ongoing experience. Usually, we become aware of growing unification over time, as we gradually come to know and accept ourselves. Our understanding of recovery develops as we apply the principles in the 12 Steps to the events of our daily lives. As we become more established in this way of life, we see that working Step 12 is not an activity to be postponed. It isn't something to be undertaken only after we have finished with ourselves.

Through the daily practice of honesty, courage, and willingness, our lives undergo a process of change. Circumstances and personalities that once seemed to dominate us gradually cease to do so. New opportunities present themselves because addictions no longer cloud our thinking. Through living in recovery, a new strength and hope grows in us.

Strength in recovery no longer depends on only us and our personal power. Strength now is fashioned from the spiritual tools we are learning to apply in our lives. Going through the Steps, talking to a trusted friend, reaching out for spiritual help—these are the sources of power that come to replace the dogged resistance or defiant attitudes of the past.

Hope, too, ceases to be a kind of wishful thinking to avoid facing reality. Nor is it the fanatical, closed-minded dedication to ideals it may have been in the dysfunctional past. The hope we share in recovery is realistic. It's based on what we see demonstrated in our lives and in the lives of those around us. Hope is restored, becoming a quality that radiates through us as our lives become meaningful and sane. In recovery, we can share hope because our lives are living proof that hope is warranted.

One of the ways we directly share our experience, strength, and hope with others is through sponsorship. Sponsorship or co-sponsorship is a committed relationship with another member of a 12-Step program, focused on applying the 12 Steps to daily life. Sponsorship involves making a commitment to working the Steps and supporting another in doing the same.

In the original 12-Step program, A.A., sponsoring someone usually meant starting with prospects who were still practicing alcoholics and sticking with them as they sobered up. In the early days, it was not uncommon to take a newcomer home, as part of sponsoring, and then to take him to A.A. meetings until he got the program. Such practices still occur. But going to this extreme is not a requirement for sponsorship nor are such practices necessarily wise or helpful under most circumstances. Facilities and professionals in the field are generally better equipped to handle intervention or direct treatment than private individuals. Sponsors don't sober people up, get them off drugs, or get them to face a self-defeating, codependent pattern. Sponsors share what they have learned with people who already have made a decision to work on their issues. We do not lead each other in 12-Step programs; we travel side by side.

In 12-Step programs today, there are many kinds of sponsorship relationships. Some contain very structured agreements to meet or talk on the phone a specified number of times per week or month. Others' arrangements may be less specific, with phone contact on an as-needed basis. Often, regular attendance of a group may be a part of sponsorship commitment.

Because individuals who have already worked the Steps may be in short supply in newer groups and because sponsors may easily become authority figures, some 12-Step programs advocate co-sponsorship relationships. In co-sponsorship, two or more people establish an agreement to work through the Steps together even if neither has done so before. Step study groups, in which a definite commitment (usually six months or a year) is made to meet regularly to work the Steps, are typically co-sponsorship arrangements.

Sponsorship is a form of putting something back— a major feature in 12-Step programs. Working through the Steps alone is not as effective as interacting with someone in a relationship of trust. Step 5 cannot be worked alone at all. Trust in at least one other human being is necessary for getting well.

There are also other ways, in addition to sponsorship, to carry the recovery message. Service work in 12-Step programs is another way to give something back. Helping to set up the meeting, sharing in the responsibilities that keep the group going—all these activities are performed by volunteers. These Service jobs are rotated among members. Aside from a few simple guidelines, any member who is willing is welcome to serve the fellowship.

In communities where the 12-Step programs are very active, an office may be staffed to do the clerical work, answer the phone, write letters, or keep regular hours for a fellowship bookstore. Tradition states that, although we may hire workers to do these necessary jobs, no one is ever paid to share their story with a newcomer. When it comes to reaching out to newcomers, this 12-Step work is done by volunteers.

Some individuals feel comfortable speaking anonymously at open meetings or in front of civic groups. Sharing our personal story in the community can be an enriching experience. Agreeing to staff a 12-Step phone line for a few hours a week is another opportunity to share in the spirit of anonymous giving back to the program. Simply volunteering to drop off meeting lists and pamphlets at public health agencies is another quiet way that gratitude and good will can get translated into action.

12-Step programs try to emphasize anonymity at the level of press, radio, TV, film, or in situations where what is said is likely to be reported. In sticking to this anonymity principle, vying for leadership among 12-Step program members is minimized. Professional therapists and others in the public eye who wish to carry the message by sharing their own recovery story sometimes aren't sure if they can do this without breaking this tradition. One way is to talk about self-help without specifying 12-Step fellowships. Another way, often used by professional therapists who are also program members, is to talk about the 12-Step programs from a professional point of view, without indicating that they, themselves, are members.

In working Step 12, we remind ourselves that little is to be gained—or given—if service or sponsorship activities become a distraction that takes the focus away from personal recovery. After all, we didn't join a 12-Step program to become an expert on how other people ought to do it. As vital as it may be that we give something back, we need to take care to balance Twelfth-Step activities, making sure that giving does not become controlling or "playing the big shot."

Our own lives continue to remain the central focus of recovery, no matter how long we've been around. Service activities may be an obvious way to practice the principles in the 12 Steps, but service isn't an escape from our other responsibilities. We must seek the guidance we need to keep our priorities straight. If our personal lives do not reflect the spiritual principles we practice in recovery, we simply have no recovery to give away.

Distancing or shutting off connections to the past may be a temptation. Sometimes it may be appropriate to put up very concrete limits and boundaries to shield ourselves from abusive situations, at least for a time. However, our issues have to be faced, if only a little at a time. Those who have attempted to deal with a problem by getting rid of it generally find that similar issues arise again and again. Internally, patterns that connect us to disturbing interactions continue to play out until we finally embrace the lesson that is there for us.

Difficult as it may sometimes be to see a path through personal dilemmas—especially those with deep roots in the past—a solution will come if we will focus on living our program one day at a time. Here are some guidelines:

1. We live only today. If something is before us that needs to be done, now is the time to do it. If we are waiting for a better time, we are missing an opportunity.

2. There's only so much we can expect to do today. Someone said, "Doing a big project is like eating an elephant; you can only do it a bite at a time!" When problems or projects tend to become overwhelming, a day at a time (or an hour at a time) can bring the project back to what is manageable.

3. Nothing lasts forever. No matter how troubling a situation may be, remember that this, too, will pass. We are not condemned to endless struggle, pain, or everlasting remorse. Neither can we depend upon having it made forever, no matter how great a present triumph. It has been said that change is the only dependable constant.

4. We can start again. Living one day at a time gives us the great freedom to begin anew, whenever we believe it is advisable to do so. We are not stuck with our patterns of error, however ingrained. We can start a new day right now and let this day make a difference.

If we make an effort to live a day at a time, we are unlikely to lose our way for long, however inclined we are to stray. Achieving lasting freedom from the pain of addictions and codependent patterns is possible. Those who choose to stay with recovery and who try to practice these principles see the benefits in their lives. Sharing the 12-Step message isn't like trying to sell something or convincing others that the 12-Step way of living works. What we share, we share out of our gratitude and from a sense of appreciation for what has freely been given to us. In trying the 12-Step method for recovery, we've personally seen that "It Works If You Work It!" And so, we think, will you.

Questions to Ponder

1. What is a spiritual awakening in your life?
2. Do you feel you carry the message in ways that are honestly you?
3. How is your program of recovery alive in you and in your life?
4. Are there aspects of your life that your program presently misses?

Other Titles in the Same Series
by Book Faith India

Pocket Guide To Acupressure Points For Women ... Cathryn Bauer
Pocket Guide To Aromatheraphy .... Kathi Keville
Pocket Guide To Astrology .... Alan Oken
Pocket Guide To Ayurvedic Healing .... Candis Canin Packard
Pocket Guide To Bach Flower Essences .... Rachelle Hasnas
Pocket Guide To Chakras .... Joy Gardner-Gordon
Pocket Guide To The Tarot .... Alan Oken
Pocket Guide To Visualization .... Helen Graham
Pocket Guide To Stress Reduction .... Brenda O'Hanlon
Pocket Guide To Shamanism .... Tom Cowan
Pocket Guide To Self-Hypnosis .... Adam Burke
Pocket Guide To Fortune Telling .... Scott Cunningham
Pocket Guide To Chinese Patent Medicines .... Bill Schoenbart
Pocket Guide To Crystals & Gemstones .... Sirona Knight
Pocket Guide To Hatha Yoga .... Michele Picozzi
Pocket Guide To Herbal First Aid .... Nancy Evelyn
Pocket Guide To Macrobiotics .... Carl Ferré
Pocket Guide To Meditation .... Alan L. Pritz
Pocket Guide To Naturopathic Medicine .... Judith Boice
Pocket Guide To Numerology .... Alan Oken
Pocket Guide To Good Food .... Margaret M. Wittenberg

For catalog & more information, write to:
PILGRIMS BOOK HOUSE
P. O. Box 3872, Thamel
Kathmandu, Nepal
Tel : 977-1-424942, 425919
Fax : 977-1-424943
E-mail : pilgrims@wlink.com.np
Website : www.pilgrimsbooks.com